About Island Press

Since 1984, the nonprofit Island Press has been stimulating, shaping, and communicating the ideas that are essential for solving environmental problems worldwide. With more than 800 titles in print and some 40 new releases each year, we are the nation's leading publisher on environmental issues. We identify innovative thinkers and emerging trends in the environmental field. We work with world-renowned experts and authors to develop cross-disciplinary solutions to environmental challenges.

Island Press designs and implements coordinated book publication campaigns in order to communicate our critical messages in print, in person, and online using the latest technologies, programs, and the media. Our goal: to reach targeted audiences—scientists, policymakers, environmental advocates, the media, and concerned citizens—who can and will take action to protect the plants and animals that enrich our world, the ecosystems we need to survive, the water we drink, and the air we breathe.

Island Press gratefully acknowledges the support of its work by the Agua Fund, Inc., Annenberg Foundation, The Christensen Fund, The Nathan Cummings Foundation, The Geraldine R. Dodge Foundation, Doris Duke Charitable Foundation, The Educational Foundation of America, Betsy and Jesse Fink Foundation, The William and Flora Hewlett Foundation, The Kendeda Fund, The Forrest and Frances Lattner Foundation, The Andrew W. Mellon Foundation, The Curtis and Edith Munson Foundation, Oak Foundation, The Overbrook Foundation, the David and Lucile Packard Foundation, The Summit Fund of Washington, Trust for Architectural Easements, Wallace Global Fund, The Winslow Foundation, and other generous donors.

The opinions expressed in this book are those of the author(s) and do not necessarily reflect the views of our donors.

CREATING VIBRANT PUBLIC SPACES

Streetscape Design in Commercial and Historic Districts

CREATING VIBRANT PUBLIC SPACES

Streetscape Design in Commercial and Historic Districts

By
Ned Crankshaw

ISLANDPRESS

Washington · Covelo · London

Crankshaw, Ned.
   Creating vibrant public spaces : streetscape design in commercial and historic districts / by Ned Crankshaw.
      p. cm.
   Includes bibliographical references and index.
   ISBN-13: 978-1-59726-482-2 (cloth : alk. paper)
   ISBN-10: 1-59726-482-2 (cloth : alk. paper)
   ISBN-13: 978-1-59726-483-9 (pbk. : alk. paper)
   ISBN-10: 1-59726-483-0 (pbk. : alk. paper)
   1. City planning—United States. 2. Central business districts—United States. 3. Public spaces—United States. 4. Historic districts—United States. 5. Urban renewal—United States. I. Title.
   HT169.U5C73 2008
   307.1'2160973--dc22   2008007568

Printed on recycled, acid-free paper ✪

Manufactured in the United States of America
10 9 8 7 6 5 4 3 2 1

Keywords: public space, urban design, historical preservation, Main Street program, parking requirements, streetscape design, town planning, pedestrian access, Lexington, Kentucky, commercial town center, human-scale design

Table of Contents

CHAPTER ONE

A Philosophical Basis for Downtown Design

Patterned by streets, shaped by buildings, and forming the connections among everything, a complex spatial fabric forms the place of our public existence in a downtown. Pedestrian walks, squares, plazas, and other intentional public spaces, street space for automobiles and buses, parking areas, transit stops, and the interstitial spaces between them all compose the downtown landscape. The design and use of this landscape have much to do with the quality of life in traditional and traditionally modeled commercial districts. Good design will facilitate movement and access with multiple modes, provide the setting for architecture, create dynamic social spaces, and contribute to the sense of center: a place where social, commercial, and institutional interaction is more dense and more vibrant than in surrounding districts.

This book draws its examples mainly from smaller cities and larger towns, but the principles apply across a wide spectrum of urban commercial districts. The central business districts of the largest cities present a distinctive set of issues related to transit, circulation, and parking that result from their singular scale and are not specifically addressed here. Even in the largest cities, however, multiple urban neighborhoods have centers of concentration where commercial and social activities are clustered in the manner of town centers.

Particularly thoughtful design is needed in downtowns because, as a human environment, they present great potential and great challenges. The viability of commercial districts is essential if communities are to offer a range of choices for living patterns. Design within them is restricted by existing spatial patterns in a way unlike few other environments. Most important is that downtowns collectively represent a vast underutilized infrastructure made up of thousands of commercial districts in towns, cities, and neighborhoods across North America. Finally, even New Urbanist commercial districts, which are modeled on traditional town centers, would benefit from careful design of downtown landscapes so that the space of these places is as varied and interesting as their buildings.

The existing development patterns of these commercial districts could facilitate a form of town life that consumes less energy and encourages better health through pedestrian and bicycle transportation. Their redevelopment and densification can help conserve farmland and wildlands. They represent a history of investment of energy and materials in buildings and infrastructure that should not be wasted. Finally, vital town centers whose historic fabric is useful in the present might enable stronger feelings of community and shared enterprise to develop.

Perhaps because they are ubiquitous, little has been written about these districts in urban design literature. Geographers, particularly John Jakle and Richard Francaviglia, have written about their evolution and meaning as places.[1] Preservationists, especially the National Trust's Main Street program, have addressed the preservation of their buildings and the financial and organizational tools that can maintain their vitality. From time to time, articles or books have dealt sensitively with design of their landscape, but generally these pieces have been issue focused or specialized in treatment.[2] New Urbanist designers credit them as models for neo-traditional communities but haven't focused enough on these places that already exist and need thoughtful planning and investment.

This book will delve into the public fabric that surrounds all the buildings and combines with those buildings to create town centers. It will discuss not only what is commonly known as streetscape design but also more: the downtown landscape's ability to provide space for the uses put to it by a town's citizenry. Streetscape design can be trivialized as a decorative effort, but it is the design of the system that connects people and places and in fact creates many of the places that make a town memorable.

This chapter describes a set of design philosophies whose application can meaningfully guide downtown design. Chapter 2 outlines spatial design issues that have been created by evolving land use patterns. The middle chapters deal with closely linked issues: the connections between neighborhoods and commercial districts (chapter 3), the analysis and design of walking routes inside commercial districts (chapter 4), and the spatial organization of parking (chapter 5). Chapter 6 concludes with design guidelines for the streetscape elements that are used to physically implement downtown plans.

In the years that I have worked with small towns—with students on university service projects, in research funded by state agencies, or with landscape architecture firms working on planning and design projects in historic commercial districts—I have been guided by some basic philosophies of landscape architecture and historic preservation. It has occurred to me over the years that these ideas are not shared by all of the different professions involved in downtown design. Certainly, the clients who live and work in small towns have a mixed level of understanding of the concepts that would enable them to communicate effectively with designers. Even many landscape architects would intuitively understand some philosophical ideas that guide their work, without being able to clearly explain them to a lay audience.

A good point to begin a book about design in commercial districts, then, is with an explanation of some of the ideas that guide useful design and that explain the very human responses and opportunities to which design is a servant. Is that not the essence of good design: that it creates opportunities for individual choice and community interaction and that it elicits responses of delight, comfort, happiness, or usefulness? That it makes new activities possible and existing activities better, more enjoyable, and more stimulating? That it allows one to lose explicit awareness of one's environment because that environment is so well suited to its purpose?

What ideas are most useful to guide design in the complex fabric of a historic downtown? It helps to look at what people do, or what they would like to do, there.

- In many towns and small cities, the downtown is the one place where people walk, not only for exercise but as a form of transportation. A downtown should be a comfortable walking place.
- Most downtowns have lost their primacy as mass-market retail districts, so they need to be engaging places for the more specialized commercial activities that can thrive in them.
- Centralized historic commercial districts are often the only commercial areas with neighborhoods in walking distance, so they need to be well connected to surrounding areas.
- These districts will not have parking directly in front of every store, as shopping centers do, so they need intuitively predictable parking systems.
- Downtowns will have the most interesting and venerated buildings, landscapes, and symbolic elements in their town. The districts need to provide a setting that lives up to their standard of quality but does not overshadow these elements.
- Downtowns usually best represent early periods of a town's development. They should be conserved so that they can continue to be part of the interesting mix of development periods found in a town.
- Finally, historic commercial districts should be places for authentic experience of what it means to be a town dweller, and they should

continue to be important places for public events, social interaction, and government facilities.

These purposes and needs that we ascribe to a downtown should be guided by principles in four basic areas. First, environments should balance between being interesting and being comprehensible. Rachel and Stephen Kaplan, in their careers as professors of psychology at the University of Michigan, have worked to understand and explain what makes environments interesting and understandable. Their book *Cognition and Environment: Functioning in an Uncertain World*, in particular, provides an excellent discussion of the balance between a level of complexity that will keep people involved in a place and a level of predictability that will help people stay oriented and comfortably master a location. Second, one should be able to feel safe and in visual control of one's environment. Jay Appleton's book *The Experience of Landscape* explains what makes people comfortable in outdoor spaces, what feels intuitively safe.[3] Third, an essential element of urban places—small town or large city—is a compact mix of land uses. Mixed land uses and short, walkable connections between parts of a town are essential for traditional town life. Fourth, rich environments result from the authentic expression of various ages of buildings and landscapes. Preservation and geography have been in a dialogue, at times an argument, over issues of the authenticity of artifacts themselves and of the life that can exist in and around those artifacts.

All of these—the need to provide comfort, the need to be interesting but understood, the need to be useful and connected, and the need to be authentic—are essential to a complete historic commercial district.

MAKING SENSE AND INVOLVEMENT

Rachel and Stephen Kaplan begin their book *Cognition and Environment* with a story.

Imagine yourself perched comfortably on the limb of a tree, peering through dense foliage at the behavior of people crossing a stream below. There is no bridge, but there are a few rocks that, with a bit of imagination, could be thought of as stepping stones. Here comes someone now. He steps out onto the stone closest to the bank, balances precariously, looks around, tentatively places one foot on the next stone, withdraws it, tries it again, and finally commits his full weight. Then more looking around, more hesitation, more testing, withdrawing, and testing again. Finally the stream is crossed, and our hero sits down on the bank for a little rest.

Now imagine another series of observations. An individual strides confidently up to the edge of the stream, steps onto the first stone with one foot, swings the other foot over to the second stone, and continues smoothly across with hardly a break in stride. There is not a trace of indecision or hesitation.

The story describes not two different people but the same person at two different times. The latter observation is of the person after he gained familiarity and became more effective in the environment of the stream crossing. The mental skill of negotiating one's way over a stream or through any physical environment requires the development of mental maps. With a level of familiarity, "a person acts as though the essentials of that environment were already stored in the head."[4]

Picture tourists driving into an unfamiliar town. As they drive into downtown, they will slow and begin to look about uncertainly, thinking perhaps about finding a parking space. They will depend strongly on signs that give directions to parking, describe businesses, or identify points of interest. There will also be familiar cues that experienced travelers will read in the environment and that will give them more confidence. Neighborhoods with older homes and perhaps tree-lined streets indicate the downtown is approaching. Street names become significant; Main, Broadway, High, and others are associated with commercial districts. As the center of downtown is approached, buildings are taller and more densely placed. A courthouse or a square may indicate the center. Certain repeated patterns help to dispel uncertainty as familiarity builds confidence.

McDonald's and other chain restaurants provide the ultimate in familiarity. The offerings and the surroundings may not be inspiring or intriguing, but the restaurant can be experienced with the confidence born of familiarity. Anticipation allows one to predict what will happen next and, in turn, what to do. Anticipation is made possible by having a cognitive map, and in the McDonald's example the diner has been allowed to form a clear map by the repetitive restaurant plan.[5]

If a person is traveling to new places or, conversely, if towns are beckoning visitors to come, how can a level of familiarity be increased? G. D. Weisman, in his research on orientation, found that structure most helped someone to feel oriented. Simple spatial structures were the least disorienting. Places with the most signs were the most disorienting because, as it turns out, excessive signs are usually used to compensate for an environment that is hard to decipher.[6]

A disorienting spatial pattern in a commercial district would likely be experienced in a typical downtown fringe. A mixture of low-rise detached buildings, parking areas, drive-through lanes, and vacant space, these areas depend almost completely on signs, arrows, and lane markings to compensate for their lack of clear spatial structure and to maintain a level of orientation. It may be that what people call ugly is simply disorienting (figure 1.1).

Figure 1.1. Green Street, Henderson, Kentucky. Without signs and lane markers, the street would have no structure that provides orientation.

Figure 1.2. High Street, Newport, Wales. A consistent line of buildings with variation provides a structure that is naturally orienting.

A downtown street defined by a consistent line of buildings provides a more orienting experience. Shop windows and signs can easily be scanned for information because they fall within a similar plane. Occasional variations in the building line are seen as significant and indicate street intersections, parking areas, or public open spaces (figure 1.2).

Skillful negotiation of the environment requires predictability; "it is said, however, that familiarity breeds contempt."[7] No town has ever printed a promotional brochure that said, "Come experience our predictable downtown!" People like variety, creating a paradox in which familiarity and variety are both preferred (figures 1.3 and 1.4).

People do not want to be overwhelmed, but they seek challenges that "fall just short of that."[8] In other words, people seek involvement in their environment.

Figures 1.3 and 1.4. Jefferson Street, Waldoboro, Maine. The two sides of the street illustrate the contrasting experiences created by streets with and without visual variety.

Figure 1.5. Wall Street, Asheville, North Carolina. A kink in the street has been made more intriguing by the design of the building facade and its entry court. It creates a destination at the place where the view terminates; at the same time, it causes the viewer to wonder what lies beyond.

Involvement and making sense are simultaneous needs. One might ask, "Is there enough order, enough regularity so that I could figure it out without too much difficulty?" And conversely, one would be concerned with "whether there seems to be enough going on to be worth further exploration, whether there is enough variety to maintain one's interest."[9] If the answer to those two questions appeared to be yes, then that place would probably be preferred.

The needs for making sense and for involvement depend on the environment for their fulfillment. The physical properties that support these needs can be identified and improved.[10] A commercial district can be analyzed with these questions in mind, and streetscape or other plans can be used to improve the situation (figure 1.5).

Legibility and Mystery

Being involved in and making sense of an environment have a present and a future component. In the present, one senses coherence and complexity in environments. Identifiability and redundance, or repeating elements, are present here and now and are the main elements of coherence. Likewise, the "visual richness or diversity of the scene" is the major element of complexity and occurs in the present.[11]

Legibility is the extension of coherence into what one imagines future experience will be like in an environment. "Environments that are high in legibility are those that look as if they would be easy to make sense of as one wandered farther and farther into them." They look as if they would allow "exploration without getting lost."[12]

Mystery incorporates complexity into the anticipation of future experience. More preferred scenes "give the impression that one could acquire new information if one were to travel deeper into the scene" (figure 1.6). [13]

In real towns, incorporating involvement and the ability to make sense requires a balance of pattern and detail, of consistency and anomaly. English author Thomas Sharp, writing ten years before the Kaplans, understood how coherence and complexity applied to both the scale of a town's plan and its individual buildings. He wrote: "There is the variety of plan-form; the variety that exists between broad

Figure 1.6. High Street, Ludlow, Shropshire, England. The shift in the street at the Buttercross creates mystery and anticipation of further movement and experience.

streets, narrow streets, different kinds of irregularly aligned streets, between open *places* compared with these, and in the differences between open *places* themselves. That is the variety of contrast. And there is besides that, and more common than it, the variety in the buildings within the streets and *places* themselves, variety that is not so much of contrast but *variety within the same kind, variety within an established rhythm,* variety . . . within similarity, within a broad unity of character."[14]

Established patterns of building widths, building heights, and window spacing allow one to establish an understanding of environmental scale and the repetition of units, and to anticipate building patterns yet to be experienced. Detailed elements of those buildings—materials, ornament, style—provide complexity and the anticipation of mystery. A similar width and spacing in windows provides consistency, but the occasional variation of a Moroccan style bay or dormers in a Mansard roof provide needed variety.

Consistency with variation naturally occurs in the design of many nineteenth- and early-twentieth-century commercial buildings. The aluminum and concrete slipcovers that were placed on Victorian building fronts in the 1950s and 1960s were removed in the eighties and nineties not only because they were nonhistoric but because they made streets boring. The slipcovered rows of buildings had no power to involve because they lacked detail and sincere variety.

The plan of streets and other public spaces in downtowns is also tensioned between coherence and complexity. A regular street grid may begin to set a pattern and to aid the sense of familiarity. A wider street, perhaps Broadway or Market, distinguishes itself as preeminent in the pattern. Perhaps a square opens off of a main street in midblock, creating a surprise widening of the open space and a relief from regularity. An extra-long block or an indented corner may provide a geographic reference point that helps one to remember locations and to give directions to others. In this respect, most American towns are balanced much more toward coherence than they are toward complexity (figure 1.7).

The town with no consistency or apparent pattern will be confusing to the newcomer. Extreme examples include the medinas, or old city neighborhoods, in North African cities, where there is repetition without regularity or hierarchy. Another is the remarkable plan of the old section of Martina Franca, Italy, with its "narrow twisted streets branching off into a hundred and sixty blind alleys" (figure 1.8.).[15]

In the United States, towns without relief from regularity are much more common, and the drabness of many towns stems from lack of variety in both street pattern and buildings. Confusingly, it all looks similar because it *is* all so similar. In towns whose problem is too much drab regularity, a streetscape plan should differentiate buildings, places, and areas by enhancing their distinctness. A plan that

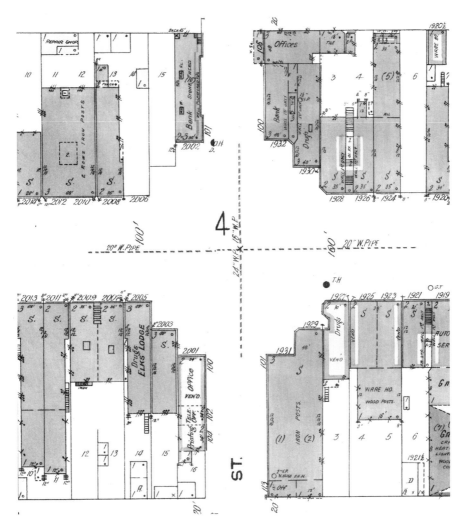

Figure 1.7. Cumberland Avenue and Nineteenth Street, Middlesboro, Kentucky. At the intersection of the two main streets in Middlesboro, the buildings on all four corners have a notched configuration, emphasizing a point of greater importance within the town's grid.

emphasized unity of materials and design treatment would only decrease the limited differences that are present. How can streetscape design enhance irregularity? Part of the potential is in architectural expression, which can be encouraged through design guidelines that emphasize expressiveness over unity. Another way to increase visual variety is to design each public space as a distinct entity and with a clear purpose, and to use different streetscape elements in different parts of a commercial district (figures 1.9 and 1.10).

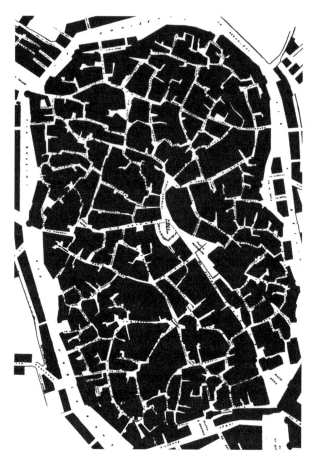

Figure 1.8. Martina Franca, Italy. The plan of the medieval section of the town creates an interesting and endlessly varying street experience. With little hierarchy, however, the experience can be disorienting.

PROSPECT-REFUGE THEORY

Prospect and refuge is a theoretical idea that explains deep-seated human environmental preferences. The theory was developed most fully by Jay Appleton in his book *The Experience of Landscape.* In short, it is based on the idea that humans feel most comfortable in an environment that allows them partial concealment and protection (refuge) while affording views into surrounding and adjacent spaces (prospect). The natural environment that best exemplifies the concept is a clearing in a wooded area. A preferred place for a person in that environment might be just inside the edge of the trees, offering concealment and views into the clearing. If one were to project this human back a few thousand years in time, the clearing and his or her position within

Figure 1.9. Main Street, Ellsworth, Maine. A business enlivens the street wall with an exuberant surface applied to what had been an unremarkable building.

Figure 1.10. Festival Plaza, Auburn, Maine. The plaza is a public space with a distinctive design that serves several purposes, including daily use and public events. (Photograph courtesy ICON Architecture)

it would clearly offer an advantage for hunting and for protection from enemies. This preference, ingrained into human minds over thousands of years, has come forward in time and manifested itself in aesthetic preferences (figure 1.11).

The romantic English landscape garden is the landscape model in which the idea is most easily seen. Prospects are open and panoramic, with clumps of trees that "open and close as one passes." Curving paths and drives offer vistas that are "deflected by their curving form." Horizons have varied profiles of "open and arboreal surfaces."[16]

Placement of tree clumps and belts creates a sense of connected irregular clearings. The clumps of trees are particularly effective as refuge symbols "firstly because they were placed irregularly within the design, secondly because they were of irregular shape, and thirdly because the individual trees were arranged irregularly within them."[17] All of these variations create a sense of a refuge that can be easily penetrated (figure 1.12).

Perhaps its ability to satisfy the preference for environments of both prospect and refuge is why the English landscape garden has remained a model of landscape aesthetics for so long. Landscapes that appear "'natural'" and that provide a mix of open panoramas, clearings, and irregularly shaped wooded areas have been consistently ranked highly in visual preference surveys.[18]

Figure 1.11. Stourhead, Wiltshire, England. According to prospect-and-refuge theory, a preferred position is looking out from the edge of a woodland into a clearing.

Figure 1.12. Woodstock, Oxfordshire, England. The park at Blenheim exemplifies the creation of a designed landscape in which multiple opportunities for refuge are visible.

Prospect and refuge can be seen in another common place: calendar photographs. Calendar photographs of landscapes, "from their inclusion in such a publication, are likely to be generally regarded as attractive."[19] A look through a Sierra Club, Audubon Society, or other calendar quickly reveals the power of prospect and refuge in our visual preferences.

How does prospect-refuge theory apply to urban streets and our preferences within them? Most people aren't consciously thinking of hiding, fighting, or running. They are interested, maybe not even consciously, in feeling comfortable. Most of the time, these feelings simply occur to us as aesthetic preferences. We think a place looks better, more comfortable, or more inviting.

A street that affords a high degree of refuge would have a street wall that appears to be easily penetrated and a sheltering edge that continues with few interruptions. A street that affords a high degree of prospect would have reasonably open views along its length and would perhaps connect into other open spaces.

Refuge

A permeable street wall is punctuated with alcoves, doorways, windows, and window displays. The doors actually allow a person to slip out of the street and into a building at many locations. More importantly, though, they and the other openings contribute to a sense that one is not isolated in the clearing of the street but has connections with the space of the buildings. One is not on stage. Permeable street edges are enhanced by variations in building setbacks that diminish the hardness of the edge. The amount of variation does not have to be great to positively affect comfort level in the street. A ten-foot-wide area that is planted or used as a sitting space between a sidewalk and a building front is a significant opening in an urban setting. Even the space created by a recessed doorway is enough to create comfortable edge variation.

A monolithic building without openings creates no refuge and makes for the distinctly uncomfortable feeling of complete exposure, of feeling as if walking naked down the street. Reflective or deeply tinted windows that allow those inside a building to look out without permitting views into the interior can amplify the discomfort by increasing the sense of exposure (figures 1.13–1.15).

An edge, along with permeability, should have continuity if it is to provide refuge. The edge of a clearing would not be much use to an ancient hunter if it was broken by large expanses of open ground. The street edge, too, provides increasing levels of comfort when it is continuous in its shelter. Continuity is most simply provided by a compact pattern of buildings adjacent to the pedestrian paths. Where there are breaks in buildings, or where they are deeply set back from the street, reinforcement of the street edge can maintain continuity. Planting, walls, or fences are some devices that may be used to build continuity.

Large open areas adjacent to pedestrian paths allow complete exposure and reduce the sense of refuge. Completely open street corners with good sight lines for automobile drivers but with no edge development for pedestrians create a loss of refuge at the precise place where pedestrians are most likely to be standing still and reacting to environmental comfort.

The sheltering ability of the edge builds up in layers. The foundation is a continuous edge that has a vertical dimension—buildings and curbs, for example. Elements that extend over the person on the sidewalk begin to create a sense of being contained within the edge space. Awnings have historically served this function as they also protected pedestrians from rain and sun. Overhanging signs and other building projections can perform the same function, if they are repeated frequently enough. Street trees provide overhead enclosure and in some places could be considered a substitute for lost building awnings. On the street side of the pedestrian walk, parked cars build another layer by creating a variable visual edge and separating pedestrians from moving vehicles. Parking meters, street lights, utility poles, bollards, trash containers, plant containers, and other street furnishings all may contribute complexity to the edge that is extended beyond the buildings to the curb.

Figures 1.13, 1.14, and 1.15. Broadway, Lexington, Kentucky. Opaque walls without openings, transparent walls with few doors, and transparent walls with multiple doors illustrate different levels of permeability on the street edge.

Figure 1.16. Limestone Street, Lexington, Kentucky. Streetscape elements that are thought of as "unattractive" may actually enhance a sense of refuge.

Some elements that are commonly considered clutter in a street environment actually enhance the sense of refuge. Large projecting signs, fire escapes, and utility poles and lines all can contribute to the complexity of an edge and are frequently seen in historic photographs of street scenes filled with people (figure 1.16).

Prospect

Prospect allows clear observation of one's surroundings. An environment with a high level of prospect has few hidden areas. The need to observe people in one's vicinity can clearly go beyond psychological comfort and be directly tied to personal safety. Walking down a dark alley that has a sharp turn concealing the other end affords no prospect and would be perceived as a dangerous environment. But even in normal, less threatening situations, a prospect is much desired.

Prospect is enhanced when views extend into adjacent spaces, such as the view from a street into a town square. As the prospect of the square opens, the observer is placed in control of a larger clearing. The prospect along a downtown street into a tree-lined residential area affords a sense of environmental connection and an understanding of the links between districts. Landmark buildings, monuments, or other elements can enhance the sense of prospect by pulling one's view farther into the distance and by giving meaning to spatial zones (figures 1.17 and 1.18).

Figure 1.17. Park Street, Woodstock, Vermont. A single landmark can extend its visual influence throughout the space that contains it.

Figure 1.18. Wall Street, Asheville, North Carolina. A clock tower designed as part of the street face for a new parking garage provides a landmark that exerts some visual pull toward the edge of Asheville's commercial district.

The ability to protect and partially conceal while allowing clear views affects the comfort of public squares and parks just as it does for streets. The ideal public plaza or square has a complex edge that provides seating or gathering spaces that are collections of coves, subareas, or territories.[20] These might be defined by walls, water, planting, paving, or other elements. A successful urban park might provide seating under a tree canopy with a clear view and connection to pedestrians passing by on a sidewalk (figure 1.19).

Spaces that are too confined, or too removed from streets, diminish visual connections and prospect. Spaces that provide too few opportunities to exist along an edge, and to feel sheltered by it, diminish their ability to provide refuge.

The two most uncomfortable and psychologically threatening spaces in a downtown are likely to be a sidewalk running between an arterial street and a large expanse of parking, and the interior of a parking garage. The sidewalk offers absolute prospect but absolutely no refuge, and the parking garage offers refuge but very limited prospect. Each space owns half of the prospect-refuge equation, and each space is completely imbalanced. Environmental balance occurs only when both prospect and refuge are proportionate.

Figure 1.19. Fifth Third Bank Plaza, Louisville, Kentucky. Edges, subareas, and prospect to the sidewalk help make a well-used public space in Louisville.

HISTORIC DISTRICTS, INTEGRITY, AND AUTHENTICITY

Most historic commercial districts are also National Register historic districts. Because they are distinguished as officially "historic," expectations of integrity and authenticity surround them. The concepts of integrity and authenticity are similar, with integrity having a much more settled definition within preservation practice. Authenticity offers a focus for healthy debate about the intended and unintended consequences of preservation and design in historic environments.

Integrity

Integrity in downtowns results from the intact condition of individual buildings along with the intact condition of the entire assembly of buildings, streets, and public spaces. The formal spatial qualities created by the relationship between buildings and open space are as essential to the character of a district as are individual buildings' designs. The National Register of Historic Places defines a basic element of integrity to be that a property retains "the essential physical features that enable it to convey its historic identity."[21] For integrity to exist in a district, "the majority of the components that make up the district's historic character must possess integrity even if they are individually undistinguished. In addition, the relationships among the district's components must be substantially unchanged since the period of significance."[22]

Downtowns are resistant to wholesale loss of integrity because they are large, are complex in form, and represent many different individual economic interests. Decisions are made by a variety of individuals for different reasons, so change happens more slowly than in less complex sites or districts. One building can lose its historic integrity and have only a marginal effect on the district of which it is a part. How much of an effect one building can have depends not on the exact fraction of total building mass that it represents but on the visual or symbolic significance it had in the original equation and on the visual power or symbolic significance of the remaining buildings. A character-filled county courthouse that is demolished to make way for a bland replacement may represent only a small percentage of the total building area in a downtown, but its removal as the symbolic focal point makes for an outsized loss. On the other hand, several well-scaled but unexciting new commercial buildings could replace older buildings and if the remaining historic structures are distinctive enough, the overall loss for the entire downtown district may not be great. The major negative impact on integrity is the loss of buildings that are not replaced at all.

Authenticity

Authenticity is conceptually related to integrity but puts a finer point on issues of character and fidelity to historic material. Authenticity is the state of being real and genuine, and not false or copied. The nineteenth-century critic John Ruskin and the designer William Morris, who together founded the Society for the Preservation of Ancient Buildings, were as concerned about authenticity as they were about the overt destruction of buildings. Ruskin contrasted what he saw as authentic use of the past on the European continent with the self-conscious preservation of sites in England:

> Abroad, a building of the eighth or tenth century stands ruinous in the open street; the children play around it, and peasants heap their corn in it, the buildings of yesterday nestle about it, and fit their stones into its rents, and tremble in sympathy as it trembles. No one wonders at it, or thinks of it as separate, and of another time; we feel the ancient world to be a real thing, and one with the new. . . . We, in England, have our new street, our new inn, our green shaven lawn, and our piece of ruin emergent from it—a mere specimen of the middle ages put on a bit of velvet carpet to be shown, which, but for its size, might as well be on the museum shelf at once, under cover. But, on the Continent, the links are unbroken between past and present.[23]

The central dilemma of preservation is this: preservation is motivated by the urge to maintain something with authenticity, but the act of preservation creates varying levels of artificiality in the artifact. The original creation will not stay original forever. It will decline to ruin or demolition, it will be repaired or restored, or it will be modified in response to some new and perhaps equally authentic need. Ruskin would probably argue that honest contemporary modification using contemporary technology and aesthetics would be preferred over self-conscious preservation intended to freeze an artifact to the time of its conception.

David Lowenthal, in *Age and Artifact: Dilemmas of Appreciation*, describes three levels of appreciation for historic sites: (1) recognition and celebration, (2) maintenance and preservation, and (3) enrichment and enhancement. Each level of appreciation has unintended (and sometimes intended) consequences that reduce the authenticity of historic places.

Recognition and Celebration

Recognizing a place as historic sets it apart psychologically from its context. The place is seen not for its beauty and intrinsic interest but in a more academic light, to be compared with others of its kind. We speculate whether it is more or less historic or interesting than similar examples.

> When we identify something as old or value its antiquity we proclaim its provenance: here, we say, is something early (or original, authentic, ancient). And so we mark the site. Designation serves both to locate the antiquity on our mental map and to dissociate it from its surroundings. It is no longer just old, but "olde." The marker emphasizes its special antique-ness by contrast with the unsignposted present-day environs, and diminishes the antique artifact's continuity with its milieu.[24]

In the Bluegrass region of Kentucky in the early 1990s, a large brown sign was placed on Interstate 64 announcing the upcoming town of Midway as "historic." The sign on the interstate carried an implication that the town exemplified Central Kentucky history, but other nearby towns protested that they were equally historic as, if not more historic than, Midway and that the town deserved no such recognition. In fact, most of these towns predated "historic Midway" by a good fifty years (figure 1.20).

Figure 1.20. Midway, Kentucky. The huge "Historic Midway" sign sets expectations for the town that it is different from "normal."

The sign was emblematic of something that was happening more broadly in Midway. The town was well on its way to converting from a locally based commercial center into a tourism, antiques, and gift economy. Compared to all the towns that surround it, Midway had made the most concerted and aggressive effort to develop tourism based on its downtown and on its connection to the horse country around it. Other towns also incorporated tourism-based retail into their downtown commercial economies, but only as a part of a mix that included local commerce and governmental services. The sign soon came down, but Midway continues to communicate in many other ways that it is a place apart from other towns in its region.

Maintenance and Preservation

Maintenance and preservation are a second level of appreciative intervention, and they introduce overt physical change. That physical change will inevitably take away some level of authenticity or genuineness. No matter how carefully thought out, preferences for particular historic time periods, biases toward certain styles, and the building technology of the period in which preservation takes place will have a standardizing effect. It is hard to resist the urge to improve on the original model: "Unfortunately, through much of the United States and in Canada, the tools we use to guide work on Main Street have promoted design coherence—even virtuosity—in formal terms, in achieving 'unite de style' on Main Street, while the qualities that inspired communities and designer—the diverse, ever-changing mix of expression, mood and activity that characterize Main Street—have too often been thoughtlessly effaced by the Main Street designer." The methods of these projects lead to a "similarity of expression" that can cause the response: "Ah, a Main Street town."[25]

Enrichment and Enhancement

The third level of appreciation—enrichment and enhancement—consciously removes evidence of the past or present and replaces it with a preferred version. The formal garden at Ashland, the estate of Henry Clay in Lexington, Kentucky, is a small example of this phenomenon. Remnants of a flower garden on the grounds and evidence in historic documents indicated that the Clay family and later owners of the property had a fairly simple but geometrically arranged flower garden to one side of the large rear lawn. The small scale of the garden was in keeping with the pastoral effect intended by the nineteenth-century design of the grounds. In the late 1940s, the Lexington Garden Club voted to construct what they thought was a more appropriate garden for the likes of Henry Clay. In a way, they decided what the Clay family *should* have had. They commissioned the design and construction of a beautiful walled garden with formal beds of boxwood and flowering plants on the site of what had probably been a livestock pen or a large vegetable production garden. The

"Williamsburg style" period garden has no historic connection to Henry Clay but aided a contemporary group in a process of myth enhancement while giving a horticultural focus to the estate. They chose "heritage" over "history" (figures 1.21 and 1.22).[26]

Richard Francaviglia, author of *Main Street Revisited: Time, Space, and Image Building in Small-Town America*, uses the example of Medina, Ohio, to illustrate this process taking place in a historic commercial district.

Figures 1.21 and 1.22. Ashland Estate, Lexington, Kentucky. The garden at Henry Clay's estate is a testament to the power of the Colonial Revival movement to enhance a landscape in a way that lessens its authenticity. The sign in the garden reinforces as fact a landscape manufactured to support a myth.

Medina has indeed become something of a stage setting in that new construction mocks the old, which is to say, a number of the buildings around the
square may look old even though they were built just a few years ago. Service
stations and buildings housing services that were less attractive—and less cost
effective in an area of increasing rents as restoration proceeded—have actually
been torn down as property values increased for lots facing the historic square.
On their sites one now finds new buildings built to look historic. These may
deceive the current visitor into thinking that the entire townscape is Victorian
in appearance and always has been since the 1880s. In fact, new construction in
Medina has filled formerly open gaps in the townscape and also removed some
less attractive or unappealing buildings that did not appear to be historic.
Some critics felt that urban revitalization in Medina had turned into preservation frenzy. . . . Thus the visitor to the square in Medina today sees a townscape that is actually more Victorian in appearance than it was in the Victorian
period![27]

Contemporary Nostalgia

There is a fourth level of appreciation that goes beyond Lowenthal's description:
completely contemporary environments are created to simulate the ambience of
idealized historic places. Based in nostalgia but unwilling to accept tawdry reality
mixed in with gauzy images of the past, these developments dive even deeper into
the world of make-believe.

The town center of West Clay, a neo-traditional development north of Indianapolis, is a newly built environment that challenges concepts of authenticity. Two-
and three-story buildings modeled on late-nineteenth-century commercial architecture were built as a retail center for the development. The block of buildings and
their parking street are positioned within an open green area that separates them
from the residential area. The commercial buildings imitate the older small towns
that can be found near West Clay, but the context for the downtown is completely
missing. There is no street grid connecting directly in all directions to the neighborhoods, no transition from high to low building heights, and no gradual change in
building spacing and density. As one drives by on a nearby county road, the effect is
much like seeing a movie set constructed in the Indiana cornfields. As the development matures, more context—houses and street trees—will develop, but there will
surely never be a burger shack, pool hall, used car dealer, or any of the other less gen-
trified elements of downtown context (figure 1.23).

The downtown buildings of the late nineteenth century were themselves revival interpretations of earlier architectural movements. Is West Clay any different? If it does lack authenticity, or is indeed outright fakery, perhaps that is only the

Figure 1.23. West Clay Development, Carmel, Indiana. West Clay's downtown is a facsimile of nearby, much older towns.

business of those who have built it and those who are buying what was built. But what is truly unfortunate is that those who crave a traditional small-town atmosphere do not infuse their economic resources into existing nearby towns.

The whole-cloth replacement of a deteriorated environment with a picturesque and historicist new one in an *existing* town is where the slope gets most slippery. The proudest example of the process is the town of Helen, Georgia. This mining and lumbering town had a hardscrabble collection of concrete-block downtown buildings in the late 1960s and appeared to its business owners to be on the verge of death. They hired a local man named John Kollock to redesign the town. He had been stationed in Germany and developed a Bavarian theme for the town's buildings and landscape. The existing buildings were renovated to the Bavarian theme, and visitors began coming. The idea snowballed: cobblestone alleys and new "Bavarian-style" buildings were built, and now Helen is the third most visited place in Georgia, behind Atlanta and Savannah (figure 1.24).[28]

Perhaps what the citizens of Helen did was the only alternative to allowing their town to die from terminal ugliness and economic decay. Anyone could sympathize with them for desiring to keep their place alive, and they have been remarkably successful. The broader effect, however, is that citizens of other towns visit Helen and

Figure 1.24. Main Street, Helen, Georgia. Helen's downtown has a Bavarian theme that was developed because a local citizen had visited Bavaria.

conclude that their town could also use a theme. Instead of discovering the character-defining elements that already exist and could be preserved and built around, they begin to imagine a whole-cloth transformation.

From the complete transformation of Helen, Georgia, to the simple identification of Midway, Kentucky, authenticity and the transformation of environmental meaning are worth considering when growth and positive change happen in commercial districts. How is authenticity maintained when "even to appreciate the past is to transform it?"[29]

That quest is not as diabolical as it may seem. Honesty, clarity, and recognizing that change is inevitable are required. The practice of preservation is based on an ideological construct that is clear in theory, if not always in the field. Careful documentation allows the preservation and replacement of material as near the original as possible. If that is not possible, and more dramatic transformation is to take place, the imprint of the contemporary period is unequivocally left. Both choices avoid the confusion created by using falsely historicist elements. To stubbornly demand complete authenticity in every action or inaction is impractical and paralyzing. Inaction resulting from a fear of change will lead to the complete loss of resource integrity as a nonadaptive downtown slides into irrelevancy and is slowly demolished piece by piece.

Revitalization: Conflicting Relationships among Design, Preservation, and Authenticity

"Many of the Main Streets that are so admired today, and that are the target of improvement strategies, are themselves the product of similar campaigns a century or so ago."[30] The City Beautiful movement spawned similar campaigns for small-town improvement at the end of the nineteenth century. Landscape architect John Nolen was known in particular not just for designing new towns but for "remodeling" existing small cities in the early twentieth century.

The themes with which we are familiar have changed little in one hundred years. In 1889, the Austrian author Camillo Sitte, in *The Art of Building Cities*, decried the monotony of contemporary towns: places that were "badly conceived settings and awkward surroundings" for public buildings and public life. In a study funded by the United States government in 1912, political scientist Frederick Clemson Howe wrote that "the American city is inconvenient, dirty, lacking in charm and beauty because the individual landowner has been permitted to plan it. . . . There is nothing to awaken love, affection, interest." In 1945, an English-language translation of Sitte's book was published in the United States. In the introduction to that translation, Ralph Walker identified "monotonous building lines, the endless streets, the rigid gridiron, the small amount of open space [of the] engineer controlled city" as the result of a "poverty of imagination" that led to the "ugly city." The problem as Walker saw it was "how to take the deadly gridiron plan and remold it into a greater freedom and a larger quality of community integration."[31]

From a pure design standpoint, most North American commercial districts still have some distinct flaws. The streets of most are intensely linear, without clear closure at their ends. Parks, squares, or other spaces that provide variety and focus may not exist. Many lack clear landmarks. Most are decidedly not green in appearance or function. Given the desire to enhance historic districts, many of these historic flaws are considered open for correction in downtown revitalization projects. In essence, desires based on honest and well-intentioned design motives come into conflict with desires based on honest and well-intentioned preservation motives.

Nodalism

One powerful design motive is the desire to enhance existing nodal spaces or to create new ones where none exist. In our imagination, the ideal small town centers around a comfortable nodal space, such as the park or courthouse square that centers so many towns in the midwestern United States (figure 1.25).

Popular movies that project an image of the ideal small town focus on this kind of space. The films *Back to the Future, The Flim Flam Man, My Dog Skip*, and

Figure 1.25. Paoli, Indiana. The courthouse square is an archetypal nodal space in a small town.

Pleasantville all used the town park or courthouse square to symbolize the essential American small town. Given the powerful imagery of what a town should be, and the desire of designers to establish order and hierarchy in urban design, the natural reaction to the many linear towns without clear nodes is to design space that provides a sense of centrality.[32]

When centrality is intended to function for the entire district, it may take the form of a new public square or park. Given the constraints of existing building patterns, it may not be possible to establish centrality for an entire commercial district. In those cases, the continuous linear system of the street may be divided into a series of shorter segments using curb realignments, planting, and other streetscape elements that emphasize the separation of blocks. These shortened segments may then each be provided with some small nodal space to center their identity. In smaller commercial districts, the entire district may be reinforced as its own node. Closure and edge may be provided at the borders of the commercial district to replace the green border historically provided by nearby residential districts.

Landmarking

Kevin Lynch's influential book *The Image of the City* articulated the importance of landmarks to the imageability of town centers. Lynch recognized that a sequence of landmarks "facilitates recognition and memorization" of routes. A series of landmarks in a district or on a route "calls up anticipation," "triggers specific moves of the observer," and gives reassurance.[33] Landmarks also provide a symbolic image that can be used as a shorthand to identify a district or a town. Consider how many towns use a local landmark, such as a courthouse clock tower, as the central image of their letterhead design (figures 1.26 and 1.27).

When clear landmarks are not present in a district, it is a normal design move to provide them. Like the methods for creating a greater sense of nodality, landmarks may be singular—a new building, a tower, or another feature that becomes a symbolic center point—or they may be distributed in the form of public art or wayfinding features, or by emphasizing and revealing existing characteristics. According to Richard Francaviglia, Walt Disney stated regarding the design of Main Street USA in Disneyland that there should be a "wienie at the end of every street."[34]

Unity, Repetition, and Rhythm

A downtown district, as the product of individual decisions made over a long period of time, possesses a strong trend toward variety. The street pattern, local preferences for building materials, pressure to conform, and architectural responses to climate are countervailing forces acting toward unity. Economic forces of the past half century that caused the demolition of traditional buildings that were replaced by parking lots or parking-oriented buildings tipped the scales beyond variety into something closer to disunity. A response of streetscape design has been to use lights, trees, banners, and other streetscape elements to reestablish unity through rhythm and repetition. Such an approach can help provide continuity of street patterns as well as the sense of refuge once accomplished by buildings and their awnings, but there is a danger of standardization implicit in districtwide treatments.

Beautifying/historicizing

In his essay "To Pity the Plumage and Forget the Dying Bird," J. B. Jackson noted that "much of the American landscape, even in prosperous areas, is neglected and mismanaged," yet common reaction focuses on appearance rather than on social and economic revitalization.[35] Issues of parking, accessibility, the inadequacy of utility infrastructure, or legal and financial barriers to building occupancy may be real problems for which beautification is proposed as an answer. It is like breaking one's leg and going to the doctor for a face-lift. While distracting attention from more sustainable and serious solutions to functional problems, beautification also affects authenticity because "beautification has long functioned as a historicizing influence."[36]

"When the recognizable past falls short of our historical ideals, we remold it to our desires. Old landscapes, buildings, and artifacts are decorated, purified,

Figures 1.26 and 1.27. Greenville, Ohio, and New Berne, North Carolina. Both towns have highly developed landmarks anchoring important thoroughfares. The fountain in Greenville is at one end of Main Street's commercial district. The steeple in New Berne creates a landmark for a pedestrian walk from a parking area onto Pollock Street.

homogenized, emulated, copied."[37] The process of beautification applies the taste of a group of people and of a particular time to a situation that is the product of diverse individuals and multiple time periods. Although community decisions must be made about community property, such as the streets of a commercial district, those decisions should be made carefully to avoid sacrificing individuality in favor of a preferred imagery.

Utility Lines, Signage, and Other Building Attachments

Examine any photograph of a commercial district from the beginning of the twentieth century. Utility lines define the overhead space of the street like the warp of some great weaving. Huge signs are painted on or project from buildings. Fire escapes, awnings, and other necessary hardware clutter the facades, especially the upper levels. These are part of the reality of historically vibrant commercial centers. But "commercialism," signage, and utility lines are rarely represented or imagined as historic elements in contemporary depictions of historic commercial districts.[38] Like a county fair's midway, which seems vibrant and exciting at night when filled with a crowd but looks tawdry and neglected by day, these streetscape elements are not usually considered worthwhile contemporary elements of a town in its current and less active condition. In the reaction away from the disarray of a cluttered townscape, variety and interest might be sacrificed along with those things that really should go.

Regional Character and Image Expectations

"The most dramatic and sustained resurrection of a symbolic landscape has been in the Main Street movement."[39] Historic preservation in the United States is most active, and has its most effective concentration, in commercial districts. The National Main Street program and other programs modeled on it are affecting thousands of smaller cities and towns. The impact is positive in economic, social, and environmental improvement. Yet, it also has its costs. The words "Main Street" carry specific imagery whose sources are regionally limited. When resurrecting towns, a great temptation exists to more closely align them with narrowly defined symbolic landscapes. Three symbolic landscapes (and there must be others and variations) that affect beautification strategies are the New England village, the Ohio town,[40] and the Southwestern pueblo.

The Ohio town is most widespread as a type and is most directly connected with the shared image created by the words "Main Street." This powerful model is based on "a street, lined with three or four-story red brick business blocks, whose rather ornate fenestrations and cornices reveal their nineteenth century origins." Although this town form symbolizes the most "typically American"[41] of towns, other historic commercial districts do not resemble it.

Many towns in the Northeast, the Mid-Atlantic, and the earliest settled parts of the Ohio Valley may lack a highly defined street corridor and a strict separation of commercial and residential building types. In the southern Appalachian region, commercial centers may be a loose aggregation of one- and perhaps two-story buildings with tenuous connections to neighborhoods. In the Midwest and the West, towns may center on a square containing a courthouse or a park and do not have a street corridor as the dominant downtown space. The buildings of many towns in the Great Plains are exclusively one story and on wide streets. And the buildings in many of these towns may have been constructed in times other than the decorative High Victorian period. In these and other town forms, authenticity resides in their own particular arrangement of buildings, streets, and spaces.

A long-standing trend to use revitalization to nudge towns closer to the Ohio norm, or to any other regional image, affects the authenticity of their architecture and landscape. Design motives and the spaces, elements, and materials that result from those motives should be carefully considered.

Authenticity of Relationships

Preservation and revitalization affect the authenticity of physical artifacts—buildings, monuments, and individual landscapes—in direct ways. Their specific authenticity derives from the amount of original material and workmanship remaining, the presence of modifications over time, and a lack of self-conscious restoration of historic features and finishes that have been lost at some time.

More subtle are the ways that preservation activity can alter relationships between historic downtown districts and their contexts. Is a district seen as a vibrant, living, working component of a town? Does it serve the contemporary needs of residents? Does it represent the aspirations and material expressions of many generations, including the present one?

The act of designating a historic district brings to bear economic and governmental forces that separate the district from its surroundings and give it a separate financial and material future. The process of drawing boundaries for the district becomes, in itself, a self-fulfilling prophecy. Boundaries are required to be "clear, logical, and defensible," but boundary delineation necessarily involves some subjectivity as decisions about including individual properties are made. "Politics, compromise, and the attitudes of property owners"[42] all may affect the outcome, because there is never an absolute line between what is historic and what is not. Once boundaries are fixed and accepted, however, they have a very real effect on the future of those areas included in or excluded from a district.

Perceptual Future

Boundaries are drawn around preferred space and also around preferred times or an "apex period."[43] The history that a district portrays is selected and boundaries are drawn to exclude other historic periods or themes. "Their definition causes historic districts to stand out as distinctive entities, sometimes more so than in their original 'historic' phase."[44] "As regimes of control and protection take effect, the contrast between the two sides of the markers becomes more and more evident."[45]

Financial and Material Future

Historic preservation tax credits apply only to buildings and districts listed in or eligible for the National Register. Although they have occasionally been created for "marginal places," design guidelines apply most often to core areas and neighborhoods where the intention is to preserve rather than to change. Revitalization projects and state funding programs for revitalization usually require boundaries that define the building resources of highest quality and leave out areas with few historic resources or where extensive deterioration has occurred. All of these financial advantages for historic districts are helpful, but they can also have the unintended consequence of growing a rose among thorns.

Areas of parking or marginal uses at the edge of a commercial district can create "border vacuums and discontinuities of use, and in places where these may do the greatest and most gratuitous harm."[46] The excluded area is often used to supply the contemporary needs of the historic district. Parking lots, banking, fast food, and other auto-oriented uses are retained and developed in the peripheral area. Governmental financial assistance to improve the aesthetic quality of streets, parking lots, and other public areas is more difficult to obtain, and private incentives, such as the federal tax credits for rehabilitation, apply in the designated district but not in its surroundings.

An excerpt from a downtown historic district nomination that is used as a model example by the National Park Service makes the point clearly.

> Excluded from the district are other areas of historic Taylorsville where small pockets of historic buildings and individual buildings have been isolated from the district by non-historic construction. The historic development along Main Cross Street north of Main Street was considered for inclusion in the district but determined ineligible. Although the area contains a number of historic and contributing buildings including the Taylorsville Public Library, All Saints Church, and some historic houses, the large percentage of non-historic and other non-contributing buildings along the street makes it a poor representation of the historic character of the town.[47]

In other words, the area left out of the proposed district is the area most in need of assistance. Along with being a "poor representation" historically, it is probably a poor human environment in which the few remaining good buildings are isolated by desolate parking lots and leftover space. But the effect of district designation will be to allow this area to continue to weaken, even as the designated area improves.

The length of the discussion of authenticity reveals the complexity and ambiguity of the issues. It can be discussed forever, but what can be done about it? The answer is not so much about doing but about being aware of the effect that design decisions will have on public perception of the history of materials, spaces, and relationships. Straightforward ideas about honesty of presentation and style can maintain a high level of artifact authenticity while accommodating change. Rebuilding deteriorated areas that lack historic resources can restore a level of contextual authenticity to a commercial district. Reconfiguring the economic role of a downtown may have implications for authenticity, but the greater risk is to stubbornly demand authenticity in every action or inaction and thus suffer a complete loss of resource integrity as an irrelevant downtown is slowly demolished.

NEW URBANISM AND OLD TOWNS

When the prophetic urban critic Jane Jacobs wrote in 1961 about "border vacuums" and other areas that cause disjointed relationships between the places where people live and the places where they engage in commerce, she was advocating an organic immediacy of connections.[48] Her call for the lively mixing of activities and people went largely unheeded for decades. The New Urbanist vision was the first popular articulation of a physical planning concept that placed major emphasis on issues of connection and immediacy.

New Urbanism and Connectivity

New Urbanism is a design and planning school of thought that applies urban design ideals said to be derived from analysis of historic towns and neighborhoods to the design of new towns and neighborhoods. Much criticism has been heaped on New Urbanism for being too idealistic in not recognizing the powerful appeal of contemporary car culture, for being a cosmetic treatment that makes urban sprawl appear more palatable, and for creating towns and neighborhoods that work for only the upper middle class. The New Urbanist ideal clearly overromanticizes the living conditions in towns that predate the automobile age. No historic town was ever as self-consciously pretty as New Urbanist places are, nor was its pedestrian system as well designed and comfortable as it could have been. Whether or not these criticisms are justified, examining the principles developed by the movement is instructive because they describe a popular ideal for traditional community form. Their prescription for building an ideal new town closely parallels a commonly accepted vision of the most positive aspects of older communities.

An advantage of New Urbanist principles is that they are pragmatic and measurable. They amount to a loosely defined pattern book for urban design. Given the patterns' basis in traditional towns, they are useful not just for designing new towns but for evaluating old towns. The patterns are undeniably attractive; the question is whether traditional towns really work that way, and if not, how much they would have to change to fit the patterns. Only an individual analysis of a given town can answer those questions for the specific place, but the patterns are summarized below and subsequent chapters describe some ways that communities deviate from them. Six patterns from the Charter of the New Urbanism specifically apply to the redesign of historic downtown streets and public spaces.

The Charter of the Congress for the New Urbanism

The Charter of the New Urbanism sets out basic principles that the Congress for the New Urbanism believes are essential for creating good towns and for remaking existing towns. Six of the principles—quoted below—directly relate to the design of commercial centers.[49] The text in italics further describes the specific application of each pattern to existing towns.

- "The development and redevelopment of towns and cities should respect historical patterns, precedents, and boundaries." *Historic preservation should be an important ingredient in a commercial center. Old buildings, patterns of land use, public spaces, landmarks, views, and other elements should be respected.*
- "Neighborhoods should be compact, pedestrian-friendly, and mixed use." *Residential space should be mixed within commercial centers. The neighborhoods surrounding a commercial center should be liveable, well maintained, and well connected to the commercial area.*
- "Many activities of daily living should occur within walking distance, allowing independence to those who do not drive, especially the elderly and the young. Interconnected networks of streets should be designed to encourage walking, reduce the number and length of automobile trips, and conserve energy." *Barriers of parking lots, drive-through businesses, and poor-quality streets and walkways should not*

discourage pedestrians from nearby residential neighborhoods from walking into a commercial center. The design of street corridors at the transitions between residential and commercial districts should be designed to encourage walking. Auto-oriented development should not expand the distance between commerce and residences.

- "Concentrations of civic, institutional, and commercial activity should be embedded in neighborhoods and districts, not isolated in remote, single-use complexes." *Government institutions, such as post offices and libraries, and the retail needs of daily life should remain in town centers for accessibility by those who cannot or choose not to drive.*

- "A primary task of all urban architecture and landscape design is the physical definition of streets and public spaces as places of shared use." *Design for pedestrians should be as important as design for automobiles. Driving, parking, and walking should be all viewed as part of a continuous experience; each part requires good design.*

- "[D]evelopment must adequately accommodate automobiles. It should do so in ways that respect the pedestrian and the form of public space." *Logically organized parking and clear access to it are essential to vital commercial centers. Parking should not dominate the form of a commercial district but should be fitted into it in nondestructive ways.*

- "Streets and squares should be safe, comfortable, and interesting to the pedestrian." *Pedestrians' experiences in public spaces should make them want to be there. They should be sheltered from sun and rain if possible, should feel buffered from moving automobiles, should have a varied visual experience, and should feel well oriented within their surroundings.*

In essence, a town aligned with New Urbanist ideals will possess the following characteristics: the infrastructure will allow for multiple modes of movement and will provide true pedestrian environments; land uses will be mixed or closely adjacent, so that various activities of daily life will be housed near one another; streets will possess high visual and spatial quality; and transitions between neighborhoods and commercial centers will clearly connect the two.

STREETSCAPE DESIGN GOALS

The intellectual foundations of city planning, landscape architecture, architecture, historic preservation, and geography intersect in historic commercial districts. This chapter's review of critical ideas from those disciplines gives a sense of the thoughtfulness that should guide downtown design. A thoughtful approach, however, must be translated into goals for action if it is to provide useful design direction. At the risk of oversimplifying the diverse issues present in different towns and cities, the following goals represent a manifesto for streetscape design rooted in preservation values.

- They will possess a balance of complexity and legibility so that they will be engaging places for the more specialized commercial activities that can thrive in them.
- They will enhance the psychological security of pedestrians with appropriate levels of prospect and refuge opportunities and will provide comfortable and accessible walking space.
- They will maintain the integrity of their buildings, spaces, and artifacts so that different periods of their histories are adequately represented.
- Their physical artifacts, buildings, and spaces will be carefully adapted over time to reflect new social and economic needs without artificial reference to historic periods.
- They will be authentically important centers for their town that do not have an artificial existence as tourist-only destinations, they will be connected to the rest of the town, and they will provide opportunities for public events, social interaction, commerce, and government.
- They will be physically connected and proximate with neighborhoods and will provide clear and useful links among transportation, parking, and places of destination within their commercial centers.

Space and Land Use Configuration in Historic Commercial Districts

CHAPTER TWO

Beginning a plan for the future of a town is like beginning an analytical courtship: it is a process of discovery. What is a town all about, and how did it get that way? What were its early influences, and how did it get to be in its current form? How does it work now, and what are its opportunities for the future? These questions are important whether planning streetscapes, parking systems, infill strategies, or public spaces. A town's evolution must be clearly understood to effectively plan for change in the future. To do this requires stepping back from isolated objectives and taking in a view that is wider across time, space, and expertise.

It is easy for one's background, profession, or intended purpose in planning to limit the view of the place to a narrow topical focus. A traffic engineer may focus solely on efficiently moving vehicles, a landscape architect on design of a pedestrian streetscape, an architect on a municipal building, and a parking consultant on parking management. Any one of these projects could be important, perhaps critical, to a town. They all need to be enmeshed, however, within a wider view, one that takes into account all of the issues, all of the known limitations and opportunities possessed by the town center and by which all of the other specific projects can be coordinated. This is a town's responsibility: to understand its own history and form so that consultants and projects can be guided by a cogent long-term view.

Understanding how a place arrived at its current state is a way of revealing its potential and its limitations. Understanding the evolution of a town's urban form and character requires uncovering the changing relationship among plan, architecture, and landscape. This chapter describes some ways in which those relationships that create town character can be followed over time both to see how a town has changed and to be able to critically examine its present conditions. The chapter begins by discussing some information sources available for mapping and describing downtown landscape history. These sources are then applied to a group of towns that exemplify the typical formal and functional divisions that exist in most commercial districts. Finally, methods for divining and recording character are considered in the hope that they can be used to make that elusive trait more tangible in designing and planning downtowns.

INFORMATION SOURCES

In most towns, contemporary spatial information is available from city governments and increasingly from Internet sources. Base maps of current conditions can be created from aerial surveys that show building footprints, street edges, and other features. Supplemental information can be developed from digital aerial photography available at no cost from commercial Internet sources and from state geographic information offices.

More effort is needed, however, to map and describe the historic and evolving spatial form and character of a commercial district. Historical spatial information comes from many sources and can lead to fascinating journeys of discovery. Town plats, town and county atlases, Sanborn maps, aerial photographs, and ground-level photographs are among the more commonly available sources of historic spatial information.

Historic Town Plats

Town plats, both the original plats and later additions, are like the architectural plans for a building. They reveal the original spatial idea on which a town's form was based and can help explain the origin of contemporary spatial organization. This information is not always of practical value in making design decisions, but at the least it can help designers understand the historical significance of certain street networks, block configurations, and interrelationships with natural features. These historic organizational ideas may help with conceptual design decisions about land use, infill locations, and the creation of public spaces. The example of Frankfort, Kentucky, described below illustrates that town plats can directly affect contemporary design that respects a historic idea.

The people who first conceived of a town may have responded to an area that they considered a favorable site and then laid a new plan upon it. Water sources, terrain, or transportation routes may have influenced the location of a town center, the orientation of streets, or the placement of a public square or other important sites.

Other town founders may have responded not to a site—in fact, they may have never even seen it—but to an expeditious plan for subdividing and marketing land. Even that relatively unconsidered process was an important decision that locked in aspects of form that affected the shape of everything to come. For example, Indianapolis, Indiana, was located without regard to specific site characteristics but in what was thought to be the center of the state. A powerful diagram emanating from a center point was created by surveyor Alexander Ralston, who had served under L'Enfant when the plan of Washington, D.C., was laid out on the ground.[1] Ralston's plan for Indianapolis ignored natural conditions but has strongly influenced the form of the central city to the present day. On a much smaller local scale, hundreds of towns in midwestern and western states were surveyed by railroad companies and laid out according to stock plans. The "Associates," a group of investors who also happened to be directors of the Illinois Central Railroad, used one plan to lay out thirty-three different towns along their railroad.[2] For good effect and bad, the grid networks on which these towns were based largely control their present form (figure 2.1).

Town plats contain simple information: street rights-of-way and lot line locations. Even this simple information can present an original intent for a town. Town plats can be found in county and city histories, and copies are also kept in county registries of deeds as references to the legal description of specific properties.

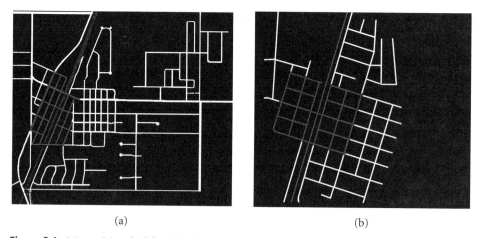

(a)   (b)

Figure 2.1. Monee (a) and Clifton (b), Illinois. The central areas of both towns are still guided by the railroad's original plan. Growth beyond the original areas varies in each town's degree of allegiance to that plan.

Frankfort, Kentucky, exemplifies the importance of original plans. The plan laid out by James Wilkinson (who a year later was actively involved in attempting to separate Kentucky from the Union and bring it under Spanish dominion in what came to be called the Spanish Conspiracy) envisioned a public square terminating a principal street, around which the rest of the streets were organized.[3] When Frankfort was named the capital of Kentucky in 1792, the public square was designated as the site for the capitol building. A simple idea—to have the most important public building in the state clearly viewed down the length of St. Clair Street—gave dignity and clarity to the organization of the town (figure 2.2). At the same time, it contributed to the development value of the land parcels on St. Clair by making them the most desirable business addresses (figure 2.3).

Later influences diluted St. Clair Street's importance as a business address. A railroad constructed by the early 1850s was aligned along Broadway running east and west at the end of the north-south St. Clair Street and separated the business

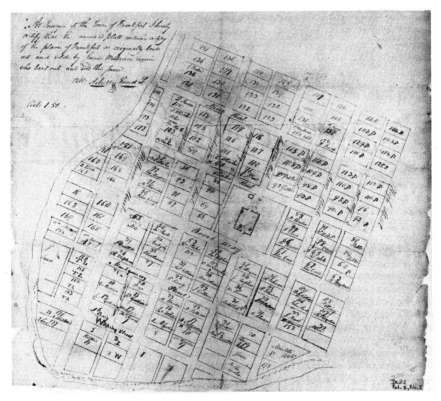

Figure 2.2. Frankfort, Kentucky. A copy of Wilkinson's original plan for Frankfort, entered as evidence in a civil trial over a property dispute, illustrates the intended visual significance of St. Clair Street, with its view to the capitol building.

Figure 2.3. Frankfort, Kentucky. By the mid-nineteenth century, St. Clair was clearly the principal commercial spine of Frankfort and was surrounded by the densest building development in the town.

center from the public square. A new capitol building was built in the first decade of the twentieth century on the south side of the Kentucky River, and a new bridge was aligned with an avenue that terminated at the new building. The railroad and the new bridge stimulated growth to the east. Eventually, St. Clair Street was no longer the center of the commercial district. A pedestrian mall constructed on St. Clair in the 1970s blocked traffic, and the mall's large trees blocked the view so that much of the planned importance of the street was no longer seen on the ground.

Figure 2.4. St. Clair Street, Frankfort, Kentucky. The view to the Old Capitol in Frankfort is restored in keeping with the intent of the town's plan.

Frankfort's plat, however, still illustrated the important relationship among the Old Capitol, the street, and the view. A new downtown plan was able to restore the importance of that relationship by reopening St. Clair Street and enabling it to link the commercial district's center with the view of the Old Capitol. This change was prompted by an understanding of the intent of the town's design gained by studying the maps that document the platting of Frankfort (figure 2.4).

County Atlases

Americans of the late eighteenth century had a passion for examining maps, viewing drawings, and reading histories of their own counties and towns. They were in this way similar to Tolkien's hobbits, who "liked to have books filled with things that they already knew, set out fair and square with no contradictions."[4]

In the post–Civil War period, the "Middle-west" in particular had arrived at a level of prosperity that must have inspired a strong sense of self-satisfaction. A new industry responded to the desire of the business, professional, and landowning classes to commemorate their own success in building farms, enterprises, and communities. An entrepreneurial system developed for publishing county atlases based on a subscription system. Atlas publishing was originally centered in Philadelphia and then spread to publishers in other cities, including New York, Minneapolis, Chicago, and Rockford.[5] Atlas publishing reached its peak in the 1880s and 1890s and gradually tapered off into the 1920s. The basic process is described in a book by Bates Harrington, *How 'Tis Done. A Thorough Ventilation of the Numerous Schemes Conducted by Wandering Canvassers, Together with the Various Advertising Dodges for the Swindling of the Public.*[6] Harrington may have considered the canvassing of individuals to underwrite an atlas to be a swindle, but these enterprising businesses created a new market and left an important historical record.

Canvassers went to a county to create maps and to seek out prominent property owners and citizens to be enrolled in subscribing to the atlas. Subscription could come in many forms. One could simply agree to buy an atlas. Escalating fee amounts purchased the display of business names on maps, a listing in a directory of businesses, or the portrayal of one's home, business, or farm in a lithograph based on a perspective drawing. Leading citizens were able (for a fee) to have their biography published or their portrait included in some atlases.

The information contained in atlases is richly descriptive and reasonably accurate but also highly selective as a result of the commercial process that produced them. The maps are the most comprehensive information included in the atlases. Most include the county as a whole and larger-scale maps of individual townships or precincts, depending on the kinds of civil divisions used in a particular state. The township maps show roads and railroads, natural features, property boundaries, and property owners' names, and they commonly represent the location of houses and other significant buildings. Town and city maps show detail at the level of individual building footprints along with business and institutional names, the layout of parks and cemeteries, property lines, streets, and other significant features (figure 2.5).

The perspective views are generally accurate representations of the form and dimension of buildings and landscapes but may be embellished in detail and finish. No corn shocks were ever so orderly, cows so content, people so well dressed, or trees so well tended as they are in the rural scenes in atlases. In street scenes, the customers are all well attired, the horses are well groomed, and the wind is blowing just right to display the flags and banners (figures 2.6 and 2.7). If such embellishment is taken with a grain of salt, however, the environmental and architectural information is fascinating and mostly accurate.

County atlases and histories are available in local libraries. More comprehensive collections for a state may be found in university libraries and state historical society libraries. The Library of Congress has a published list of the holdings under the

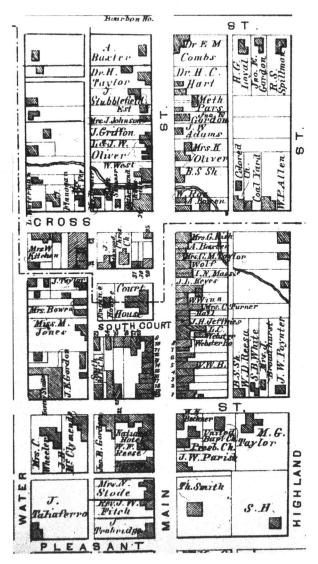

Figure 2.5. Winchester, Kentucky. The Clark County atlas contains a map of Winchester that is much like a figure-ground study, with building masses clearly delineated.

title *United States Atlases: A List of National, State, County, City, and Regional Atlases in the Library of Congress.*[7] Digital access is increasingly available to historic atlases through county, university, and state libraries. One example is the University of Iowa, which is making the content of its collection of Iowa atlases available for on-line viewing and downloading.[8]

Figure 2.6. Metamora, Indiana. An image of a farmstead from the Franklin County atlas illustrates the level of perspective accuracy combined with the embellishment of details that is typical of such pictures.

Figure 2.7. Winchester, Kentucky. Drawings such as this one from an atlas of Clark County, Kentucky, provide an accurate reference for the design of buildings and their street environment.

Sanborn Maps

Fire insurance maps were widely produced in the United States beginning in the middle of the nineteenth century. The maps were produced by independent mapping companies for sale to insurers, who used them to assess the fire risks posed by the properties surrounding an insured building. In the beginning, many companies produced maps within only their own local areas. Between 1876 and 1915, the Sanborn Map Company absorbed all of the independents and became the sole provider of insurance maps. The company eventually produced maps for more than twelve thousand towns located in every state.[9]

Information for Sanborn maps was collected in the field by the company's roving surveyors, called "striders, trotters, or pacers", who had a mandate to uphold the company's reputation for accuracy.[10] More than three hundred field employees crisscrossed the country during the years of peak production.[11] They were guided by the company's fieldwork manual, *Surveyor's Manual for the Exclusive Use and Guidance of Employees*, which stressed "uniformity and standardization."[12] The introduction explained that Sanborn maps "are made for the purpose of showing at a glance the character of the fire insurance risks of all buildings. Our customers depend on the accuracy of our publications, and rely upon the information supplied, incurring large financial risks without making personal examinations of the properties" (figure 2.8).[13]

The five hundred employees in the company's Pelham, New York, offices translated the field sheets and notes into finished products. This involved several stages of examination and proofreading intended to guarantee that Sanborn Maps were "the law concerning risks in the insurance field."[14]

The reliability of the field measurements and of the resulting maps has made them a tremendously useful resource for historic information. When compared with contemporary site measurements, Sanborn maps are startlingly accurate when one considers the number of properties that had to be measured to compile a set of maps for a town or city.

Time is another dimension that adds to the usefulness of the insurance maps: they were updated at intervals of roughly ten years from the 1870s to the 1930s, and corrections were made for some cities into the 1960s. As a time-sequenced set of planimetric snapshots, the collection of Sanborn maps for a community gives a reliable record of change in a town's buildings and urban design pattern (figure 2.9).

The availability of Sanborn maps is restricted by location. The Library of Congress has a nearly complete set of all of the maps. In most states, a paper collection of the maps for that state are kept in a university, historical, or research library. Other copies of the maps for a specific town may be kept in that town's planning or build-

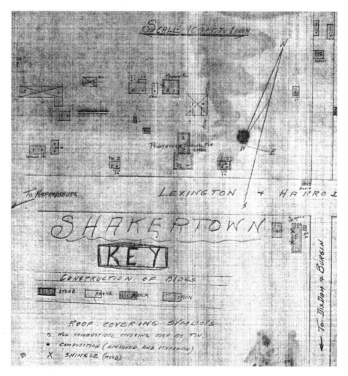

Figure 2.8. Pleasant Hill, Kentucky. The field notes prepared by a Sanborn company surveyor at the Shaker community of Pleasant Hill, Kentucky, reveal the precision with which field measurements were recorded.

ing codes department or in some other location. The locally kept maps are more likely to include pasted-on updates that obscure older building configurations. This can limit their usefulness as illustrations of a specific time period. The entire Library of Congress Sanborn collection is available on microfilm. Microfilm copies for specific areas are available in some municipal, college, and university libraries. The microfilmed copies are, however, not in color. Digital copies of Sanborn maps are available as a database service through libraries. Digital copies are black and white only, and access is restricted to that part of the database to which a particular library subscribes. For example, a county library in a particular state likely will subscribe only to that state's maps.[15]

The *Union List of Sanborn Fire Insurance Maps Held by Institutions in the United States and Canada*[16] is a comprehensive listing of states, towns, and map years with all known locations for a map set. It includes statewide or regional map collections, along with some collections in larger municipalities, but does not include most additional local locations for maps of smaller cities and towns. *Fire Insurance*

(a)

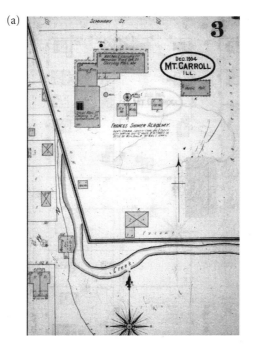

(b)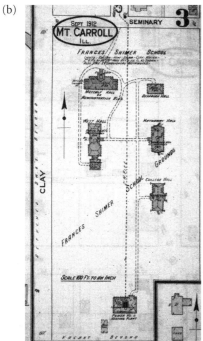

(c)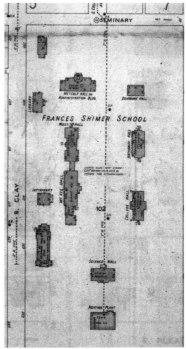

Figure 2.9. Mount Carroll, Illinois. A time sequence of Sanborn maps of the campus of Shimer College in 1904 (a), 1912 (b), and 1931 (c) illustrates the maps' value in charting landscape development over time.

Maps in the Library of Congress: Plans of North American Cities and Towns Produced by the Sanborn Map Company is a checklist of the maps in the Library of Congress collection.[17]

Historic Photographs

People have been taking photographs of their towns since the 1850s. Similar to the burst of map and atlas production before and soon after the turn of the twentieth century, the quantity of photographs of commercial centers was tied to the accessibility of photographic technology and the desire to document a radically changing landscape. The dense clustering of multistory business buildings, the development of public space, and the concentration of commercial and social activity in downtowns were remarkable to the citizens of growing towns and smaller cities between the Civil War and the Depression. In response, they took photographs or purchased them from others.

The postcard industry began in the mid-nineteenth century and flourished after the 1893 Columbian Exposition in Chicago popularized postcards. The heyday for picture postcards of commercial districts was in the first two decades of the twentieth century, when collecting postcards was a widespread passion in the United States.[18] The intent of many of the views in commercial districts appears to be to declare that the place is not quite so small, so rural, or so Podunk as one might think and to project justifiable pride in a town's area of greatest social and financial investment. The camera is usually viewing down a busy main commercial street, turned slightly toward one side to emphasize the building fronts. Views from upstairs windows or from roofs looking down onto a street are nearly as common (figure 2.10). Both views provide clear documentation of buildings, street design, trees, lights and other street equipment, and activities.

In contrast to single-source documents (such as Sanborn maps), historic photographs and postcard views are typically fairly dispersed within a community. Local libraries are the most reliable starting point for accumulating a set of photographic views. Most libraries have a photograph collection as part of their holdings in local history. Whatever their collection, the library staff is usually the best reference for locating other sources, such as a newspaper archive, a historical society, or local collectors.

Historic Aerial Photographs

Aerial views are nearly as old as photography itself. The first known aerial photograph was taken of a Paris suburb in 1858 by Gaspard-Félix Tournachon, who was

Figure 2.10. Main Street, Danville, Kentucky. Nineteenth- and early-twentieth-century street scenes were frequently shot from upper-floor windows and gave an unobstructed view of building and streetscape details.

better known by the pseudonym Nadar. Nadar was famous as a photographer and social critic, and in 1863 he became the honorary president of the Society for the Encouragement of Aerial Locomotion by Means of Heavier-than-Air Machines. Jules Verne was the secretary of the group.[19] Nadar believed in the power of flight as a tool for the cause of greater democracy and liberation, and his interest in aerial photography stemmed from its power to demonstrate the different view of the world possible from the air. His famous first aerial view, which has not survived, was taken with a large-format camera and developed in a portable darkroom in his balloon basket. "Abandoning all clothing for the sake of lightness, he ascended in a captive balloon above Petit-Bicetre, just outside Paris. Clutching his Dallmeyer camera with its horizontal lens of his own invention and concealed under a black curtain with orange blinds, he returned with a clearly identifiable image."[20] The ability to see the urban landscape from the sky created a sensation, and aerial views of urban and rural landscapes have never abated in popularity. Nadar continued to take photographs of urban Paris and to demonstrate the usefulness of flight for many years, including as a means for Paris to communicate with the rest of the world while it was surrounded by the Prussian Army in the siege of 1870–71.

Experimentation with aerial photography continued with balloons, kites, pigeons, rockets, and early airplanes until World War I. The war was the first time governments considered widespread use of aerial photographs practical. The better and lighter equipment developed for aerial reconnaissance during the war led to later peacetime interest in aerial photography for mapping and landscape interpretation. Interest centered on visual access to remote or large areas difficult to survey from the ground. By the mid-1930s, the U.S. Department of Agriculture (USDA) was using aerial photography to measure forest stands, to map soils, and to record agricultural land use. The planes flew a series of parallel lines and had no reason to alter their flight paths when they came to towns. The creation of a collection of aerial views of towns has been an unintended benefit of large-scale aerial photography of rural lands.

Some communities commissioned flights as early as the 1920s for planning purposes, but this was typically done only in larger metropolitan areas. Aerial photographs do not cover the history of most other towns before 1935, when the USDA began flying them, so they do not extend far back into most communities' histories.[21] The peak density of development in most small and midsized commercial districts, however, was in the thirties, so this was fortuitous for documentation.

Aerial photographs provide qualitative detail not available from most other plan views. Tree lawns, street trees, and sidewalks can be seen in aerial photographs but are not usually shown on other maps. The configuration of parks and other public landscapes, the location and size of parking areas, and the vegetation patterns on rural properties at the edge of a town are other examples of features best seen in aerial photographs. The book *Above and Beyond: Visualizing Change in Small Towns and Rural Areas* offers excellent examples of how aerial photography can be used in planning and preserving towns and open space.[22]

All of these sources, and others, can help one understand the evolution and significance of a town's physical form. An organizational process that sorts through, correlates, sequences, and geographically categorizes descriptive material will make the information more useful and more easily communicated to others. A basic outline for making the material most useful might be to create a time sequence based on the periods of different map sources. The maps then provide their own sequenced documentation of plan form change and, at the same time, provide a geographic reference for photographs, drawings, or other information forms. These sources can be keyed to map locations for their period and used to develop multiple levels of detail.

PATTERNS OF CHANGE

Change is continuous, but the speed of change is uneven. Towns, individually and in the aggregate, change rapidly in response to economic, social, and technological transformations. They may exist through other periods with little change. The 1880s, the 1920s, and the late twentieth century were times when transforming economic processes left clear records in the built forms of many towns in the United States.

The changing morphological characteristics of commercial centers in seventeen towns in Indiana, Ohio, Kentucky, and Tennessee were followed through these three time periods to see how their current forms compare with historic patterns of development.[23] They range in population from slightly over 5,000 to just less than 50,000. One is a neighborhood center that serves a population of about 10,000 within the city of Lexington's larger population of 275,000. All but one of the towns were formed in the late eighteenth or early nineteenth century and had an identifiable commercial district by the late nineteenth century. The exception is Chevy Chase, in Lexington, which developed as a streetcar shopping district at the beginning the twentieth century. The forms of the towns' plans are all generally gridlike but with shapes that vary from compact to linear depending on topographic and transportation influences.

Morphological descriptions of the towns were based on comparison of the spatial arrangements of buildings, streets, and other space in and around each town's commercial center over time. Information sources included Sanborn maps, USDA aerial photographs, a variety of map sources published by the towns themselves, aerial oblique photographs taken by the author, and field observation.

The decade of the 1880s was the end of the preindustrial period of landscape and architecture in the region's towns, and it contrasted to the town form and character in the first quarter of the twentieth century. Richard Lingeman called the period that bracketed the turn from the nineteenth to the twentieth century the apotheosis of the small town in America—the age of its greatest glory.[24] The current persistent images of small-town landscapes hearken mainly to the buildings and public landscapes created in that period.

By the end of the 1920s, the height of an era was expressed in the form and character of many towns. Small-scale industrialization and capital concentration caused the population balance to shift from farms to towns. The automobile was common by the twenties and allowed farmers to come into town with greater frequency and from greater distances. The automobile was part of a process at this time that led to greater urban density and a more consciously designed public environment, but it had not yet influenced the towns to the point where they lost density and design clarity in response to the decentralizing effect of automobile ownership by town dwellers.

At the end of the twentieth century, a move back toward a lower urban density was well established. Commercial patterns continued to respond to the increasing convenience of automobile-centered mobility. Accommodating the space require-ments of people who wrapped their bodies with automobiles had a serious impact on the proportion of space and building mass in towns. Despite revitalization proj-ects, the National Main Street program, and much concern on the part of historic preservationists, there remained no doubt that the centers of small cities and towns were not the dominant retail and commercial districts in their communities.

A DEVELOPING PATTERN: THE END OF THE NINETEENTH CENTURY AND BEGINNING OF THE TWENTIETH CENTURY

Town maps from the 1880s give a distinctly nonurban impression. The town centers had mixed building patterns and building uses. They were decentralized and lower in density relative to their condition in the 1920s. In some towns, the central area could not yet be described as a business district, because of the lack of concentration of businesses in the area (figure 2.11).

In towns that did have an exclusively commercial district, the buildings were smaller than they would be in the ensuing period, and typically each business was in an individual building rather than in the business blocks that would be developed later. Vacant lots still existed along with large gaps between buildings where the street frontages of lots had not been built out to their full widths.

Land use was mixed. Residences occurred in the center of town, and businesses were mixed into the residential areas. A distinct lack of unity in architectural mass-ing and patterning existed because of this land use mix, the variety of business types in any given area of the downtown, and the small scale of many of the buildings. Single-story frame buildings stood next to two- or three-story brick business build-ings, which might themselves be next to a livery yard (figure 2.12). For example, the town hall of Lebanon, Ohio, was in the dead center of town, on the corner of Broad-way and Main, but was flanked by houses and faced a third house across Main Street.

The public landscape of the period was mostly devoid of formal design beyond the simple platting of public streets, and public improvements extended only to the rude paving of streets, the construction of mainly wooden sidewalks, and the provi-sion of such utilities as water and drainage where they existed. What would later be-come Central Park in Henderson, Kentucky, was a plain public square used as an in-formal trading center, parade ground, and parking area for horses and wagons. The Larue County, Kentucky, courthouse faced three small and nearly dilapidated build-ings, which occupied the other half of the Hodgenville town square. The organized planting of street trees in the public right-of-way in the neighborhoods surrounding downtown was limited in scope.

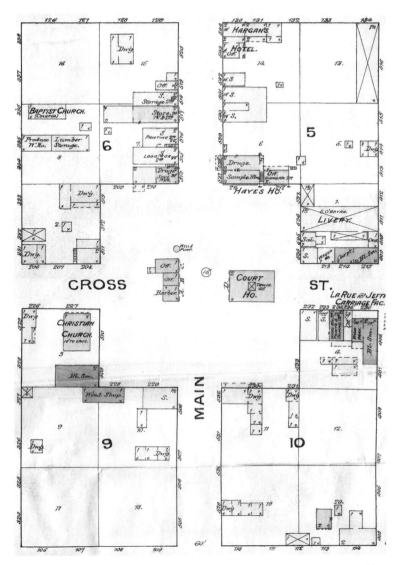

Figure 2.11. Hodgenville, Kentucky. Hodgenville's square was surrounded by a mix of houses and commercial buildings in 1886.

The edge between the commercial and residential areas of the town centers was nondistinct. Just as houses extended into the center, there was also much blending at the edges. Hotels, restaurants, and groceries extended into Henderson's neighborhoods, along with a number of tobacco stemmeries, where tobacco leaves were stripped from the stalks and warehoused. Churches and nonsecular institutions were commonly integrated into residential neighborhoods by the 1880s.

Figure 2.12. Lincoln Square, Hodgenville, Kentucky. The scale and quality of buildings could be inconsistent. Here, a small blacksmith shop stands next to a prominent bank building, which is bordered on the other side by a fenced residential yard.

Perhaps the least urban aspect of the building pattern was the spacing between residences. In most of the towns, the residential pattern was more like a village or a hamlet, with varied setbacks from the street, wide spacing, and irregular development.

The decades from the 1880s through the 1920s brought tremendous physical change as populations shifted from countryside to towns. The studied towns' populations increased by an average of 269 percent, while the populations of their states increased by only 167 percent between the 1880 and 1930 censuses.[25] Along with their increased populations, they provided an increasing number of services to their rural population base as travel into towns was made more accessible and as farmers became more specialized into cash crop production and developed a greater dependence on manufactured goods and food products. All of these factors fueled downtown growth. Nationally, the percentage of farms with automobiles increased from 31 percent to 58 percent between 1920 and 1930.[26] Such towns as Pikeville and Jackson, Kentucky, also served as the commercial centers for large populations of coal miners and their families who lived and worked in the eastern Kentucky coalfield in Pike County, Breathitt County, and other counties. This pattern was repeated throughout the country wherever resource extraction driven by industrialization created a need for new populations of workers in rural areas.

The memory of more rural patterns must have made the towns seem strikingly urban to older residents in the 1920s. Infill and replacement intensified the patterns from the 1880s to create a peak of development density. Commercial areas could not increase greatly in area because they were encircled by already developed residential neighborhoods. New business buildings were constructed on vacant lots or filled the street frontage of lots that had been previously built upon. Buildings were enlarged or were replaced with larger buildings, and the dwellings that were mixed into the business district were torn down and replaced with business buildings. Danville, Kentucky, had one of the more established commercial districts in the 1880s. It stayed within its old boundaries into the 1920s, but ground coverage by commercial buildings nearly doubled in some commercial blocks (figure 2.13).

Danville and Henderson had commercial centers that were sixteen and thirty-eight acres in size, respectively. Of this area, a third was occupied by street rights-of-way, a third was covered by buildings, and the last third represented other space within the blocks. Put another way, 50 percent of the land within blocks was covered by buildings. The contrast between building mass and void was more striking from the street than the percentage of ground coverage would make it seem. Street edges were consistently defined by buildings. The blocks in the commercial center of Franklin, Tennessee, presented building faces defining the street line for 90 percent of their total block length.

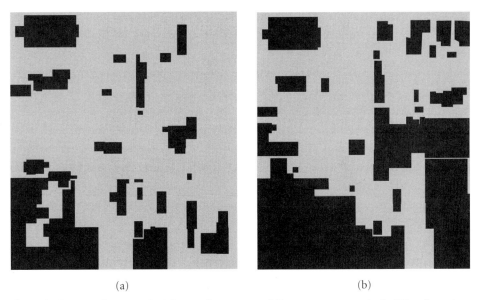

(a)   (b)

Figure 2.13. Danville, Kentucky. The two figure-ground diagrams represent the building footprints in the block bounded by Main, Broadway, Second, and Third Streets in 1886 (a) and 1914 (b). Building coverage increased dramatically and consolidated into larger building masses.

In the residential areas also, vacant lots were built on so that a more consistent pattern of residences developed along the streets. Neighborhoods were fitted tightly to the commercial centers, with no gap between. In most cases, the edge was simply the change between two properties from commercial to residential and the corresponding change in building type and relationship of building to site. Business growth into residential areas was limited to occasional house-business combinations, which were mainly professional offices or service businesses, and to a number of small groceries distributed throughout residential districts.

The towns' institutions—including churches, social organizations, and libraries—continued to be well integrated into residential areas. This gave them a reasonably central location, but without having to be in the zone of highest building density and commercial activity. The block of Main Street just north of the commercial center in Versailles, Kentucky, had a typical mix, with three churches, four large residences, and a wood shop and auto garage at the border of the downtown (figure 2.14).

Photographs and narratives reveal an aspect of use that allowed this distinct separation of mass and void to exist: the street was still a multipurpose space. Cars, and still some horses, were parked across large proportions of street width. Diagonal parking was typical on both sides and often in the middle, too. Businesses stockpiled bulk goods and received deliveries from the front. Traffic intensity and its regulation were light enough to allow diverse uses of streets.

The automobiles that brought people into town were beginning to create a limited amount of direct physical change in the form of new land uses (the automobile garage and the service station) and new street elements (traffic lights and the provision for more orderly on-street parking), but off-street parking lots were not yet necessary. It was a period of equilibrium between urban form and the car. Accessibility to the rural population brought prosperity, density, and public improvements to the town, and yet there were still few enough automobiles that they could be accommodated without seriously disrupting pedestrian environments and existing spatial patterns. Walter Kulash has called it the "first motor age," when "we did not try to rebuild our cities to accommodate cars. We thought we could incorporate cars by adapting existing street forms."[27]

Spatial Patterns: Downtown

The business districts in the early twentieth century were not uniformly beautiful, but they did possess clarity of visual structure and land use pattern.

Commerce and aesthetics were not always in opposition. Large buildings were erected that had style and inspired genuine community pride. The county

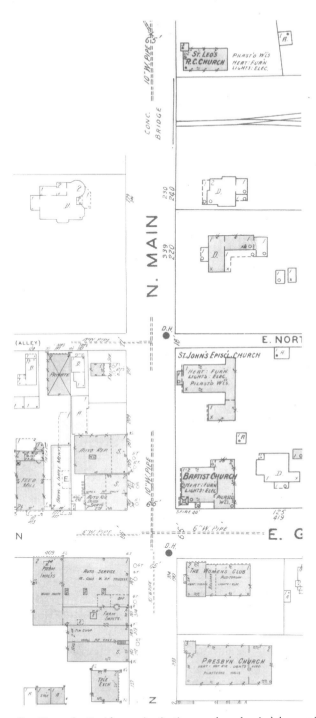

Figure 2.14. Versailles, Kentucky. Residences, institutions, and mechanics' shops mixed at the downtown fringe.

courthouses were elaborate, imposing, domed structures, many built in this period. New commercial buildings or blocks benefited from the new architecture. The Italianate style was frequently employed in the 1880s, and was well adapted to producing an elegant façade on a row of buildings, with bracketed overhanging cornices, rows of arched windows, occasional columned arcades, raspberry-brick fronts, and stone trim and ornamentation (which later gave way to cast iron and pressed tin).[28]

The essential characteristics of their visual structures were unified architectural massing and continuous patterns of building facades, open street space, and developed and ornamented public spaces.

The period from the 1880s to the 1920s brought the development of the multi-business building or "block" and the completion of the street frontage in business districts. The limited variety of materials, the similarity of building uses, and the need to provide daylight to the interiors caused a pattern of facades that may have varied in style of ornament but that were consistent in pattern and scale. Commercial buildings were uniformly built on the street right-of-way, creating a consistent wall for the street space. The increased visibility of corner lots made them more valuable properties, and taller, more ornamented buildings tended to be built on them, anchoring the ends of the blocks and providing emphasis to the corners.

The ratio of street width to building height in the central blocks varied from town to town. In Danville, with a wide Main Street, the ratio was three horizontal feet of street width for every one vertical foot of building height in the center of the downtown. This degree of enclosure was much less than most large cities of the same period, but in contrast to the open agricultural setting of central Kentucky, it provided a strong sense of enclosure. In eastern Kentucky, space for streets and buildings was more limited, and on narrow Second Street in Pikeville, the ratio of street width to average building height was one and one half horizontal feet to one vertical foot, providing more vertical emphasis to the street enclosure.

The strong enclosure provided by continuous building facades contrasted with the openness of street spaces themselves. Continuous street tree plantings were unusual in the core areas. Hodgenville was exceptional with its rows of trees on North Main Street and on the northeast corner of the square. Most downtown buildings were not designed with the intention of having trees placed in front of them. The storefront cornice or horizontal sign panel that was typically provided for the name of the business was placed at about the level where a tree canopy would hide it. The facades themselves were ornamented and patterned with the intention that they would be seen and that they would enliven the space of the street. Fixed or retractable awnings were commonly used on buildings, especially those that faced the afternoon sun, to shade pedestrians and first-floor display windows.

This design allowed visibility and a sense of prospect. At the same time, the variety of awnings and signs applied to the buildings created a degree of clutter, although nothing like the clutter of signs that would develop by the 1950s. And even with the distraction of signs and other elements applied to the front of buildings, the essential character of an open street strongly defined by a varied architectural wall was clear.

The view out of the downtown and into the neighborhoods provided the defining image of street space in the core of the town. With remarkable consistency, photographs of downtowns from this period show this core street space being terminated with trees at the edge of the adjoining neighborhoods (figure 2.15). In most downtowns, these core areas were only two or three blocks long, so the trees remained visible throughout their length. The presence of the canopy and the shadow cast onto the street provided closure to the linear space of the street and marked the edge of the residential district.

A stronger civic landscape had appeared around the turn of the century as these towns, like towns and cities all over America, became more concerned with quality of life and self-image.[29] This concern manifested itself in the coordinated planting of street trees on residential streets and in the development of public spaces. Hodgenville tore down the three ramshackle business buildings in its square to create Lincoln Square, and Danville developed a parklike entry to the courthouse, with trees and a fountain. Bowling Green, Kentucky, had developed Fountain Square in 1872 as an elaborate promenade ground surrounding a large iron fountain, and nearby towns, including Henderson, were inspired by this model to improve their own squares and downtown parks by the beginning of the twentieth century (figure 2.16).

Figure 2.15. Main Street, Henderson, Kentucky. Trees terminated downtown districts by enclosing the street space where residential neighborhoods began.

Fountain and Band Stand,
City Park, Henderson, Ky.

Figure 2.16. Henderson, Kentucky. The fountain in Central Park was typical of the effort to create more pleasant pedestrian environments in town centers at the turn of the twentieth century.

Towns all through the Midwest developed their courthouse squares or park squares as landscapes befitting the self-image of towns that had come of age. In an early example of the historicizing effect of beautification, New England towns transformed greens that had been filled with "brush, stumps, stones, rubbish, dead trees, and stagnant pools, swarming in summer with disease-carrying insects" into parks according to the Colonial Revival vision.[30]

Spatial Patterns: Neighborhood

The neighborhoods that provided the setting for the downtown core stood in marked contrast to that core. First, the volume of space that centered on the street was given much less enclosure by the envelope of building facades that lined it. Second, the street space itself was more complex, varied, and transitional than it was in the downtown.

Residential buildings were generally lower than downtown commercial structures and gave less enclosure to streets. The houses and institutional buildings of the neighborhoods had varying side-yard widths and were set back farther from the street than were the commercial buildings of the downtown core, and so they provided a less definite street facade. Setbacks from street edges were variable, with twenty to thirty feet typical. Visual emphasis occurred at those places that were exceptions to the typical setback on a given street. Shotgun houses and other small house styles commonly occurred in clusters and were set closer to the street. In contrast, the largest and most expensive homes occasionally punctuated a street by being set back farther, allowing the yard to become a more parklike space.

Buildings were not the primary enclosing element for the street in residential districts. This function was fulfilled by trees and other elements that created a more layered and complex division of space. Beginning with the paved vehicle way, enclosure was provided by street trees planted in the public tree lawn. This created a softer definition but a smaller volume of enclosure than did the buildings of the downtown core. The pedestrian walkway was also defined on one side by the street trees and on the side toward the houses by fences, low plantings, or additional trees. The yard provided a buffer to the private space of the home, and even the building itself could provide a transitional space in the form of the front porch. The effect of this multi-layered series of transitions between the public space of the street and the private space of the home was to define the street as a conduit for traffic and pedestrians and to provide a level of separation from the semiprivate space of the yard and the private space of the residence beyond (figure 2.17).

RESIDENCE SECTION, NORTH MAIN STREET, HENDERSON, KY.

Figure 2.17. Main Street, Henderson, Kentucky. Residential segments of downtown streets possessed multiple layers of space that eased the transition between houses and the vehicular way.

Spatial Patterns: Industrial and Service Areas

The use of streets as workspaces had faded by the 1920s. Industrial and storage buildings had traditionally been built on the street edge, and the public street was the only space available at the front of the buildings for outdoor activities. Tobacco wagons were parked on the street until they could be emptied into warehouses, carriage makers pulled their completed work out onto the street, and farm supply stores used the street as a loading area for wagons and trucks. With growing numbers of automobiles and subsequent traffic regulations, however, the street became increasingly reserved for vehicles in motion. Parking was restricted to specific areas at the edge or in the center of the street, and other uses were banned. When the streets were no longer available for these activities, other space had to be found on private land. Moving utilitarian uses of the street onto private lots meant that less of the lots were available for buildings themselves. The pattern that began to develop for service businesses was the one that we have today: buildings pushed to the back or to one side of the lot, with parking, loading, and short-term outdoor storage taking up the remainder of the space.

CHANGE THROUGH THE LAST HALF OF THE TWENTIETH CENTURY

If the 1920s were the height of building intensification, the 1950s began a period defined by fragmentation. A generally accepted idea in the Ohio Valley, if not across the entire United States, is that the commercial centers of small towns and of older districts within cities declined between the beginning and the end of the twentieth century. In actuality, most grew in area. They declined in relative importance, however, because by the end of the century they possessed a much smaller proportion of the building space used for the retail business than they did at the beginning of the century.

Winchester, Kentucky, for example, has about three hundred thousand square feet of ground-floor building space designed for commercial activity in the downtown area. This commercial space could easily fit within the combined floor areas of the Wal-Mart superstore and the Kroger supermarket on the bypass road.[31] Add in the other big-box retailers and the dozens of smaller stores outside of the town center, and the result is that the downtown provides less than 20 percent of the commercial space in Winchester.

In 1925, almost all retail activity in Winchester took place in the town center. The exceptions were small grocery stores scattered into the neighborhoods. The size of the downtown then was about two hundred thousand square feet of ground-floor building space. The building space has not changed dramatically since then—it has actually grown by 50 percent—but it has declined in relative proportion to the rest of the town.

The other commercial centers in the region around Winchester also grew, and continue to grow, in area. But as they have grown in area, their density has fallen. Danville and Henderson serve as good statistical examples. Both towns' commercial centers doubled in land area between 1925 and the end of the twentieth century, but the area of building coverage increased by only 50 percent in that time. The building coverage of post-1925 development was half as dense as previous development. If building height were taken into account, density would contrast even more because later commercial construction was usually one story (figure 2.18).

Building density is significant, but the pattern of building distribution in commercial center growth has had an even greater morphological impact. Buildings of the second half of the twentieth century were usually built back from streets and behind on-site parking. Street corridors are drastically different as a result. Sixty-five percent of the street right-of-way edge within the commercial area that was developed by 1925 in Versailles still has direct building frontage, whereas only 10 percent of the right-of-way in the area built after 1925 has direct building frontage.

CONTEMPORARY ZONES OF LAND USE AND FORM

Among a variety of different plan organizations in the studied towns, twentieth-century growth and change created strikingly similar patterns of land use, spatial characteristics, and street types. The major pattern of district organization in a small downtown today is a dense core area of historic commercial buildings surrounded by fringe areas of much less densely spaced commercial buildings and parking lots. How did this fringe area develop? How much of it is the result of growth into neighborhoods, and how much is the result of demolition of the commercial area? To answer this question, the building patterns of the 1920s business districts of selected towns were delineated in plan drawings and compared with contemporary plans of the same areas. These drawings revealed changes in building location and size throughout the downtowns and made it possible to determine the extent to which fringe areas had been carved out of or added on to older business districts.

Plan comparison reveals two major kinds of land use and building pattern change. One kind is that areas at the edges of the old commercial districts have less dense architectural patterns resulting from reduced numbers of buildings and

(a)

(b)

Figure 2.18. Henderson, Kentucky. Figure-ground studies of commercial development in Henderson in the 1920s (a) and the 1990s (b) reveal a doubling of land area devoted to the commercial center, but with growth taking place in a lower-density pattern. In the maps, solid black shapes represent commercial or institutional buildings, and outline shapes represent residential buildings. The gray areas illustrate the extent of the commercial district.

building square footages. The second change is that the low-density pattern is extended in area by commercial building growth beyond the edge of the old commercial district.

Three distinctive zones can be identified by mapping development change from the early and late twentieth century: the *architectural core* and the *parking and service zone* are both within the historic boundaries of the business district, and the *business expansion zone* is outside those boundaries (figure 2.19).[32]

These land use configurations apply to towns generally but are most clearly defined in larger towns, where each zone is large enough to show a repeated pattern and a distinctive character within the downtown area. In the smallest towns, the same land uses and building types happen in a similar arrangement but only the architectural core is actually large enough to possess the repetition of land use necessary to form something that looks like a contiguous district.

The zone descriptions are typical, and it is unlikely that they will match perfectly with any single town. The patterns and characteristics of land use are, however, consistent in the towns that were analyzed. The three zones differ enough in land use and visual composition that each can be described as a distinct set of characteristics. There are also characteristics that overlap zones and design issues that may apply to all areas of a downtown.

Architectural Core

Building density and the continuous street facade that were characteristic of the historic business area remain most intact in architectural cores. The architectural cores

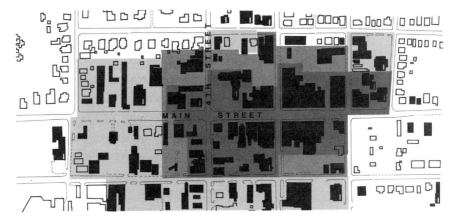

Figure 2.19. Danville, Kentucky. Commercial districts in many town centers consist of multiple functional zones: an architectural core (dark gray), a parking and service zone (medium gray), and a business expansion zone (light gray).

occupy, on average for the study towns, 55 percent of the area that was occupied by the historic business district. This zone of downtown is not always completely congruent with National Register Historic District boundaries because the architectural core can include "nonhistoric" buildings. It is the pattern of building placement and density that identifies the core. This zone is the most pedestrian-intensive part of the downtown and is the area that provides the least amount of parking immediately adjacent to its businesses. The visual imagery associated with Main Street is derived from the patterns of the architectural core, and it is here that design attention has traditionally been focused.

Spatial Characteristics

The architectural core contains the most vertically and volumetrically defined space in the contemporary downtown. The mainly continuous building facade provides enclosure to the space of the street and at the same time enlivens the street with pattern, repetition, and variety. The density of buildings, merchandise, signage, and (usually) pedestrians is another characteristic of the architectural core that is not matched in other parts of a town.

Design Issues

Most of the design issues in core areas relate to preserving their distinct building mass and street-space relationships.

Public space. Most towns have some historic public landscapes downtown. Often they have been symbolic, political, and social centers for the town. But over time, many of them have been modified for parking or other utilitarian reasons that have impinged on their ability to serve as aesthetically and symbolically significant places. Others have been victims of accretion—a monument here, a memorial there, a plaque on the street—whose cluttered landscape obscures any sense of order or design. Older public spaces should be carefully tended, with preservation or new design restoring their dignity and attractiveness as important landscapes.

Core areas can present opportunities for new public spaces. When they do, these opportunities may commonly be seen as merely ornamental in their potential and then lose the opportunity to serve a larger public purpose. If small commercial districts most often lack something, it is quality space to gather people together in groups large or small. Design of new public space should be based on functional needs.

Many core areas have narrow sidewalks and very little other room for pedestrians that is provided in a decentralized fashion. Provision for smaller "pocket" spaces can alleviate the perception of poor accommodation of pedestrians by relieving consistently narrow walks. Very small areas may actually serve most of the need for public space since small commercial districts only occasionally need to accommodate a crowd.

Corners. The loss of corner buildings is a major issue affecting the spatial continuity of the core area in Main Street towns. Corners are important to the spatial development of the block because of their ability to terminate and enclose the view from the street and because of the anchor they provide to a block of buildings. While corners were previously considered prominent building locations because of their visibility, they later became desirable locations for parking lots, service stations, and convenience stores because of their accessibility to automobiles. The greater size of many corner buildings has also hindered their preservation and continued use because of the greater amount of capital required for investment in them. When two or more corners have devolved in this way at a single intersection, the spatial structure of the street erodes. This condition is particularly prevalent at the edges of the core area, where it reduces the strength of contrast with adjacent zones.

There are other cases where corners have been maintained as open space that improves the quality of an urban landscape. These are corners whose visibility has been exploited to make a public space more prominent. Parks, courthouses with lawns, and churches are three frequent uses of these kinds of public spaces.

• *Midblock openings.* Midblock openings create discontinuity in the collective building facade and reduce street-space definition. Usually, they function as parking lots, which cause the sidewalk to become a thin ribbon of pavement between two automobile zones. In addition, the sidewalk's continuity is broken by the curb cut leading into the parking lot. In extreme cases, the openings extend all the way through the block interior to the next street. Novelist Richard Russo wrote about this condition in the fictional town of Mohawk, New York.

> With so many gray buildings gone, the town resembled a Hollywood back lot. In the gaps between buildings you could see things that weren't supposed to be visible from the street—dirty side entrances to shops that kept up halfway decent appearances out front, full garbage dumpsters awaiting trash collection, a car or two on blocks—things that would have been secrets had the buildings along Main formed an unbroken line. No doubt the back alleys of every town were more or less the same, but it seemed a shame the town should be so transparent.[33]

Such openings are one motivation for the rows of street trees planted in the architectural core areas of so many towns; the trees are an attempt to compensate for the gaps and to bring continuity back to the street.

Like open corners, some midblock openings are positive elements for the street. Openings might be well-designed passageways to parking areas in the interior

Figure 2.20. Main Street, Danville, Kentucky. Trinity Church punctuates its block with a shallow interruption in the street facade.

of blocks, planted areas that provide visual contrast, niches for sculpture or other public art, or small areas to sit or congregate (figure 2.20).

Edge and closure. The defining view out of many downtowns looks down the space of the street and is terminated at the edge of the commercial district by street trees enclosing the street in the neighborhood. In many cases, the closure to this view provided by the neighborhood trees has been lost over time. The resulting effect is that, rather than being anchored into the town, the architectural core floats visually in its surroundings.

Street trees. Street trees in architectural cores provide positive environmental qualities: they shade the walkway, give a sense of spatial buffer from street traffic, provide linear continuity to blocks in which buildings have been demolished, and—in towns where building facades have been visually simplified with aluminum or other covering systems—provide textural variety.

The other side of this equation is that street trees have not always been appropriately applied to commercial centers, nor has the architectural core provided a hospitable environment for trees. In a town with a rich variety of architectural patterns and a mostly continuous street facade, no great need exists for trees to provide linear continuity or textural variety. The need for shade on south-facing walkways has been met traditionally with awnings projecting out from buildings (figures 2.21 and 2.22).

Figures 2.21 and 2.22. Main Street, Danville, Kentucky. The environment created under a row of street trees can be quite pleasant, especially on a hot summer day. The same trees viewed from across the street, however, can obscure the buildings and signs that distinguish an architectural core area.

The problem in many towns where trees have been planted in the core area is not the presence of the trees but the uniform and inflexible way in which they have been placed. Trees are needed to carry the building facade across midblock openings and around corners where buildings have been removed. They can help emphasize the ends of blocks and provide terminus to the architectural core in places where its connection to the surrounding area has been severed. Every town has specific situations in which trees are a critical design element. By carefully considering their use and placement, trees can be a welcome presence in the architectural core and can help maintain the historic patterns of this important zone of the downtown.

Where street trees are planted, they need adequate soil volumes, the ability for oxygen and water to penetrate to the root zone, and adequate overhead space in which to grow. The degree to which these requirements are restricted places limitations on the ultimate size and life span of the tree. In many cases, the life span is so limited that trees should rightly be considered a temporary element requiring periodic replacement. Finally, trees and all vegetation should be planted and maintained with thought given to the personal security of pedestrians, especially at night. Shrubs should be low enough and tree branches should be pruned high enough to maintain clear visibility near pedestrian ways.

Isolation. Design attention in terms of building rehabilitation has naturally focused on the architectural core because it contains most of the historic commercial building stock. Design of the urban landscape has usually also focused on the architectural core, with good intentions but frequently to the neglect of the less architecturally and historically significant areas surrounding the core. A pattern is then created in which the core becomes isolated and specialized within its surroundings because the spatial structure breaks down in the surrounding areas. A major issue for maintaining or improving the physical condition of the architectural core itself, then, is developing stronger spatial connections with the surrounding areas.

Parking and Service Zone

The parking and service zone was a part of the historic business district, but a large number of the buildings that existed there have been replaced with parking lots, drive-up facilities, and service and loading areas. This zone visually appears to have lost building area, but the total amount of ground coverage by buildings has not changed significantly. The smaller number of buildings that remain are larger individually than the ones that were previously in the zone, and the process of consolidation into fewer buildings has left more open area in the zone. The zone's location generally forms a fringe around the architectural core because of its function to supply parking for the pedestrians who populate the core area. The parking and service zone occupies, on average for the towns that were studied, 45 percent of the area that was occupied by the historic business area.

This area includes larger, publicly owned parking lots as well as numerous unconsolidated, privately owned parking lots whose edges have been determined by property boundaries. Isolated business buildings and institutional buildings remain from the period when this was the edge of the historic business district. This zone is generally weak in urban design quality but is economically important for the parking it provides and for the convenience businesses, such as dry cleaners and drive-up bank branches, located here.

Spatial Characteristics

The predominant spatial characteristic of the parking and service zone is horizontality, because of the lack of elements above waist height to mark and define space. The parking lots are generally open, without tree islands or other defining elements and with the only vertical edge being the backs of buildings. Another predominant characteristic is a sense of unpredictability or disunity caused by the randomness of the overall pattern of buildings, parking lots, and other elements. Streets passing through this zone lack enclosure and definition. Many pedestrians in the architectural core either park in this zone or walk through it on the way to the core, but pedestrian amenities typically are scarce.

Design Issues

Design issues in the parking and service zone center around the need to have it function as a positive pedestrian bridge between the core and the rest of the town and to establish a street character that has continuity with the core area.

Street space, access, and pedestrian amenities. Discontinuity between architectural cores and the neighborhoods surrounding them is largely caused by the breakdown of street space in the parking and service zone. The space of the street lacks enclosure and allows open views into parking lots and the rear side of commercial buildings, thus creating a negative space leading into the architectural core.

As the area that supplies parking for many of the pedestrians in the architectural core, the parking zone should be conducive to pedestrian movement. At the most basic level, walks should be well maintained and safe, dropped curbs or other necessary features should provide for accessibility, and the negative effects of curb cuts for driveways and parking lot entrances on pedestrian movement should be minimized by consolidating entrances and continuing walkways across entrances.

Lighting that illuminates walks and parking lots and that is scaled to pedestrians is an important element that can extend the landscape design vocabulary of the architectural core into this zone. Shade trees are also an important element for pedestrian comfort in the parking and service zone. With few buildings to provide shade, visual texture, or spatial definition, trees become much more important in fulfilling these functions.

For pedestrians walking from a neighborhood to the downtown core, the street space may be a ribbon of concrete walk between the asphalt of the street and the asphalt of the parking lots. The development of planting strips, groupings of trees, architectural screens, or other kinds of buffering and enclosing elements between parking lots and the sidewalk would both give enclosure and continuity to the automobile street and provide a more hospitable pedestrian environment. The few buildings in the zone should be made a part of the street by designing an edge that emphasizes the buildings instead of screening them. New buildings should be built on or close to the right-of-way line to enhance the street edge.

Parking lot design. Parking is a predominant function of the area, yet the layout of parking is largely ad hoc. Its design often does not consider aesthetic issues, and it sometimes provides limited function. A major improvement in the efficiency, order, and visual quality of parking lots in many towns could be achieved through the coordinated layout of the many unconsolidated parking lots owned by individual businesses. In many cases, consolidation would create the same or a greater number of parking spaces and still allow for the introduction of tree islands, walkways, and other elements to humanize the parking lots. Local zoning ordinances should be considered carefully to make sure that they do not apply suburban standards for parking to downtown districts. Downtowns should be treated differently primarily because they have a higher capacity for street parking and because parking is shared between multiple properties with different peak-use periods. Tree islands help to clarify auto circulation, provide a mix of shaded and sunny parking spaces, and reduce the scale of open space in parking areas. Well-designed pedestrian walks in and out are essential to an inviting experience, and landscape and architectural features that buffer parking areas without hiding them help to integrate them into a downtown's fabric.

Simplicity and clarity of circulation are important to developing the perception of parking availability. The fact that an ample number of spaces are provided doesn't really matter when parking lots are confusing, create difficulties in maneuvering, or seem disconnected from the intended destination. Improving parking lot circulation should be accompanied by carefully considering the number and location of street entrances to maintain convenient automobile access while improving the pedestrian environment.

Expansion Zone

Business expansion zones are areas where commercial development has expanded beyond early-twentieth-century downtown boundaries. Post-1920s business development occupies nearly half of the total downtown commercial area in the towns studied. Business expansion zones are the most complex parts of downtowns because they are the result of contemporary land uses being unevenly superimposed on historic land uses. There are three subareas in business expansion zones:

- highway-style strip development
- local strip development
- house-business area.

In all cases, these commercial development areas have been carved out of or super-imposed on residential neighborhoods that surround historic business districts.

Highway-style strip development resembles that found on the outskirts and bypass roads of most towns; in the downtown, it occurs along the major street or streets that lead into the architectural core. It contains businesses that appeal to both residents and those traveling through a town and that depend on a high volume of traffic to be financially successful: fast-food restaurants, chain drugstores, and gas stations.

Local strip development occurs on secondary streets, is more destination oriented, and is not as dependent on a high volume of traffic. Business types include groceries, lumberyards, auto repair shops, professional offices, and other service businesses.

Residential-to-business conversion can occur on a variety of street types surrounding an architectural core as long as the houses in an area are substantial enough to house a business. These conversions are largely for service businesses, such as professional offices, beauty salons, funeral homes, and insurance agencies. Land use change can transform the character of formerly residential areas with signage, parking, landscape design, and the demolition of some houses for parking lots or modern building additions.

Spatial Characteristics

Spatial characteristics naturally differ in the three subareas with a descending scale of auto intensity and an ascending scale of remaining historic fabric.

Highway-style strip development. This development area is probably the most horizontally oriented of all the downtown zones. There are usually few or no street trees and very few buildings fronting immediately on the public right-of-way. Building setbacks are at inconsistent distances from the street, and typically considerable space exists between buildings. Off-street parking is usually provided in front of buildings. Parking lots are owned by individual businesses and limited to use by their patrons, but spatially they flow together with very little definition of separate parcels, contributing to the overall quality of openness. Although plentiful off-street parking is an integral part of this zone, it is not uncommon for there to also be parking on the street. Signs dominate architecture as visual features, and signs and utility poles provide the scant enclosure given to the street space.

The highway-style strip area usually has the most poorly developed pedestrian walks in the downtown. There is excessive interruption of the pedestrian way with curb cuts, and the walkway is rarely horizontally separated from the roadway.

In contrast to the parking and service zone, which possesses disunity as an unintentional product of its ad hoc development, the signs and buildings in strip developments promote intentional contrasts with each other. The public landscape contributes to this situation because, with its own lack of spatial order and presence, it is not able to provide balance to the zone.

Local strip development. Business buildings front closer to the street right-of-way in the local strip area. Signs are less dominant in this area because of the business types present in the subarea, the fact that signs are more frequently attached to buildings, and the slower pace of traffic on the streets found here. Parking is typically between buildings in this subzone. Buildings tend to be isolated from one another by the parking areas, presenting a discontinuous street facade. This area is not as horizontal in nature as the highway-style strip, but it lacks continuity.

House-business zone. With its green front yards and residential building scale, this area is unique among downtown commercial areas. The street right-of-way in this zone still typically contains a public tree lawn between the walk and the street. Street trees are more likely to be found here than in any other part of the downtown, but they are frequently in poor condition or are inconsistently planted. Parking is less extensive because the business types require less parking volume. Some disruption of building and yard patterns does occur, however, because of parking development. In some instances, this zone acts as an effective transition between downtown and residential areas.

Design Issues

Design issues in the business expansion zone relate to its improvement as an auto-dependent commercial environment that should also serve pedestrians and avoid excessive intrusion into the historic connections between neighborhoods and commercial districts.

The pedestrian in the car. The business expansion zone developed in the automobile age; it is designed for the sequence of activity in which one parks the car close to the business, conducts one's business, and then moves the car to the next place of business. The engineering requirements of the car have been accommodated, but the person driving the car experiences a visual environment with no unifying characteristics. Visual and spatial quality does not have to remain limited to the pedestrian areas of urban environments. Improving automobile environments in the business expansion zone enhances environmental quality and image within the zone and improves the link between the architectural core and the rest of the town. A high-quality automobile environment depends on street corridor development and site planning for individual properties.

Characteristic elements of a high-quality automobile corridor include buffer areas between streets and parking lots, adequate spacing between entrances onto streets, simplified signage at predictable heights and locations, lack of utility line clutter, and coordinated systems of lighting and directional signage. Improvement in the quality of the street corridor requires a mix of private and public land, investment, and cooperation.

Site planning. The business expansion zone developed lot by lot, with no unified pattern of development to replace the pattern established in the architectural core. As a result, many businesses would benefit from site planning to retrofit them into the town fabric (figure 2.23).

Elements to be addressed in site planning include the following:

Figure 2.23. Kirkwood Avenue, Bloomington, Indiana. Redesigning the sites and street edges of poorly designed expansion zone properties can help to reintegrate them into the fabric of a town center and improve the quality of the street for pedestrians.

- plantings or other landscape features to more clearly separate the parking lots of adjacent properties
- more clearly defined edges between streets and private lots
- improved parking lot design to clarify circulation, eliminate unnecessary driveways, and provide a tree canopy
- coordinated use of plant materials on different properties to establish greater compatibility and to ensure that good-quality plants appropriate to their function are chosen
- pedestrian connections to connect the public walkway and the business buildings
- future site development that places buildings on the street right-of-way with parking behind the buildings.

Building improvement. Low levels of building maintenance can create negative contrasts between architectural cores and expansion zones. Individual business buildings in expansion zones benefit from exterior rehabilitation, repair, and maintenance in much the same way that buildings in core areas do, and greater continuity between zones would also result.

Sign design. Many expansion zone businesses survive by advertising and depend on quickly recognized sign logos to identify themselves. Chaotically organized and competing signs, however, produce a negative image of business quality, and they conflict with unified landscape development. Sign design should be compatible with the different subareas in an expansion zone. The scale of signs should reflect that they are read by both pedestrians and automobile drivers. Sign characteristics that, if coordinated, would lead to greater cohesion in the zone include size, height, distance from the street right-of-way, quantity of information, and placement relative to street trees, light standards, and other features. These sign characteristics should be coordinated in concert with the other features of the street, while the individual graphic design should continue to express differences in color, shape, and graphic elements.

Public signs detract from the visual quality of the expansion zone as much as private signs do in some towns. Public directional, informational, and regulatory signage should be rationally organized to reduce clutter and to increase quick comprehension.

Parking redundancy. Parking is one of the most sensitive issues in historic commercial districts. Almost no one would accept the idea that there is more parking than necessary in a downtown. The issue is where the parking is located relative to the destinations generating the traffic. In some cases, parking spaces are underutilized because of a surplus in a particular location, even when the overall situation is a parking shortage. This surplus happens most frequently in the business expansion zone, particularly in the highway-style strip area.

It is in places where off-street parking lots are combined with on-street parking that the spatial quality of the street corridor has often deteriorated the most. On-street parking in the highway-style strip area has frequently been developed on what was a public tree lawn when the zone was residential. The need for buffer areas between the street and private parking lots could be satisfied by restoring the tree lawn. Where this is not feasible, the alternative for establishing buffer areas is to go outside of the public right-of-way.

Parking placement in the house-business subarea. Parking development in the house-business subarea sometimes follows a pattern where one house is developed for the business and the neighboring house is torn down for a parking lot. In other cases, a large residential lot is purchased on which parking can be developed next to the house. The typical businesses in this area do not depend on high client turnover and are not high-traffic, impulse-driven businesses. Although parking must be adequate, the need for parking to be highly visible is not important, because visits to these businesses are usually planned. Developing parking areas behind buildings would reduce their visual impact. Constructing or planting adequate screening around parking areas closer to the street would also minimize their impact and reinforce the street space.

Residential landscape and street trees in the house-business subarea. Some of the best downtown tree-planting sites and other opportunities for more varied planting are located in the house-business subarea. The area commonly offers wide public tree lawns and front yards. Unfortunately, these spaces are not always well planted. The three greatest problems are poor tree maintenance, failure to replace trees that have died, and poor tree selection. Good tree maintenance includes removing damaged limbs promptly, not allowing the top of a tree to be butchered, and protecting the base of the tree and its root zone. In an area with a residential pattern of building placement, streets benefit from consistent street tree patterns that give enclosure and character. Replacement of dead trees is essential to maintain the pattern.

Choice of tree species deserves careful consideration. It is not a good idea to create a monoculture of one tree species throughout a town, but some consistency in form and size is appropriate on a street or in a neighborhood. Small tree species cannot frame streets with a green canopy. Rather, they present a mass of foliage at a low height that can obstruct visibility and require pruning to avoid conflict with pedestrians or parked cars. Larger trees shade a wide area of street, walk, and yard; enframe streets; allow buildings to remain visible; and maintain the historic character of residential streets.

PLACE: SPACE AND CHARACTER

The preceding sections have discussed a functional land use approach to analyzing spatial configuration and associated design issues in historic commercial districts. This last section discusses the less tangible aspects of place, space, and character.

If streetscape and other design work should reinforce individuality in the character of a town, how does one discover and describe that character to begin with? No answer to that question will satisfy completely or apply everywhere. Documenting building ages and styles and mapping land use and building types get at elements of character but fail to describe perception—the experience of how it feels to be in a particular place at a particular time.

The meaning of the term *place* is both multifaceted and contested. Place is, as Delores Hayden says, "a suitcase so overfilled that one can never shut the lid."[34] It may be a physical reality described in sensory terms that relate it to an individual viewer at a given time; it may exist as memories of experience; it may have very little to do with the formal qualities of physical space and instead be the creation of social relationships and patterns of activity; or it may be a symbolic state of being, as in "to be in one's place."

For our purposes here—to inform decisions about design that will improve a town's ability to thrive as a place to live and work—place is most productively viewed as a physical reality in the present. In this view, each town is a phenomenon that unfolds to the person experiencing it in a way that is distinct in some ways and similar in some ways to other towns. If place is indeed a phenomenon, then it is not merely a set of concretized forms and volumes—it depends on the movement and experience of a viewer to make it real. It cannot be studied in maps or from remote office spaces only. To analyze place requires an experiential approach that involves movement through the place(s) in question—what Gordon Cullen described as "serial vision."[35] The intent of this kind of analysis is to absorb sensual knowledge of the environment and to describe and define those elements that make it distinctive, pleasing, intriguing, off-putting, inviting, hostile, beautiful, ugly, enclosing, opening, unifying, and diversifying.

If place were viewed as a pure phenomenon, then a common understanding of the place characteristics of a particular town could never be developed—each person experiencing it would understand the place differently. There is an inherent contradiction between phenomenon as an individual experience and the need for public consensus in planning and design. How can one person's experience of place be documented, communicated, and understood by the larger group? To do this requires a method and language that is nonesoteric and reasonably universal in its terminology. Place is too important to be left out of the analysis of a town, but it also has to be dealt with in ways that can be discussed and understood in public meetings with a town citizenry.

Christian Norberg-Schulz, in the opening chapter of his book *Genius Loci*, set out the two main elements of place: "The structure of place ought to be . . . analyzed by means of the categories 'space' and 'character.' Whereas 'space' denotes the three-dimensional organization of the elements which make up a place, 'character' denotes the general 'atmosphere' which is the most comprehensive property of any place."[36] To describe place, one may begin with the foundation of space. If one has already created base maps of a commercial district and its context, and has already mapped land uses, building footprints, and other elements of the built environment, then the outline will be in place for mapping space, its volume, and the edges that create its enclosure. Space will have dimension (width and height), it will have a shape or configuration, it may contain solid masses or objects, and it may be modified by screening or filtering elements.

Each space will contain, be enclosed by, or look out to elements that establish its particular character. The quality of sunlight and reflected light; the texture and detail of materials, building patterns, plants, and pavements; and colors are recordable characteristics that create ambience. The intensity of occupancy and the types of uses to which buildings are put are elements of character that communicate social value. Building age, scale, and rhythms create patterns of character related to history and building technology. Views within the space, into connecting spaces, to distant horizons, or to nearby landmarks create kinetically evolving images that may aid in orientation and legibility.

Adjacent spaces may be similar enough that they can be combined as character areas: distinct adjacent volumes of consistent perceptual character. Conversely, a single space may have subareas of very different character that enhance its interest and complexity or create discord and illegibility.

An exercise that describes place through an analysis of space and character almost inevitably leads to an assessment of how it could be made more complete, vibrant, or distinct. In a historic commercial district, an assessment might be categorized generically as strengths and weaknesses or somewhat more specifically as conditions to be respected and conditions to be improved.

Landscape architect Harry Garnham, in his book *Maintaining the Spirit of Place*, defined several categories of special places to consider in town planning and design. He identified the following categories:[37]

- *Special streets* encapsulate the essence of a neighborhood or district.
- *Boundaries* are perceived between areas of distinctly different character.

- *Special areas* are districts with a unified positive image.
- *Buildings essential to function* establish orientation and identity for a community.
- *Buildings essential to image* are recognized elements of character because of design or siting.
- *Good views* help to establish the visual character and image of a district.

In addition to those categories, other kinds of places to consider include the following:

- *public spaces*, including parks, plazas, or the outdoor foyers to public buildings
- *monuments* or other elements that act as public or political symbols
- *natural features*, which may include specimen trees, streams, slopes, or other features
- *building configurations* where the relationship of a collection of buildings, rather than the design of a single building, makes a special place
- *gateways*, places where one senses the change from one zone or district to another
- *working elements*, which are significant because their function is essential to the place
- *small spaces and visual spaces*, spaces that may not be publicly accessible because of their scale or because they are private but that are part of the visual order of the town.

In his planning work with the town of Manteo, North Carolina, landscape architect Randy Hester found that planners' and designers' concepts of special places, like those identified by Garnham, do not always parallel the views of local residents. In developing the town plan, residents identified the places that they considered essential to the self-image and function of the town and that they thought should not be changed. One resident named this set of places the "Sacred Structure of Manteo."[38] In general, the sacred spaces were small in scale and were not those elements that would have been selected by a professional designer or planner as visually significant. They included such places as the post office, a town boat launch, and a gravel parking lot that held many town festivals and the town Christmas tree. Because they were visually ordinary kinds of places, only a few had previously been identified for protection in the town's historic preservation or zoning ordinances.

Both kinds of places need to be considered in downtown design: spaces that have identifiable spatial and visual character and those that have social attachment for the residents of a town. A town's places have contemporary value as components of a system that allows citizens and visitors to develop a mental construct of a town. They are frequently descriptive of a town's history and are connections to its evolution. Inventorying a town's places is an essential part of the physical planning process. If character and identity in a town are to be maintained or emphasized, then place must be dealt with as a significant element.

CHAPTER THREE

Connections: Neighborhood and Downtown

Strong connections between neighborhoods and downtowns are critical to vital town structures and vibrant town life. The identities of the districts mediated by a connection are defined partly by the connection itself. In a town, "no part is independent. All are interlocked, and to break connections is to injure the whole mechanism."[1]

The everyday experience of life in places as different in region and urban scale as Nevada City, California, and a New York City neighborhood depends on the adjacency that allows walkable connections between homes and business districts. One great value of living in a place like Manhattan's Gramercy Park neighborhood, and dozens of similar neighborhoods in New York, is the easy walk from one's home in a quiet enclave to the vibrant commercial life of the groceries, restaurants, and convenience stores on Third Avenue (figures 3.1–3.4).

In Nevada City and other compact towns, the scale is smaller, but one can walk downtown to a smaller-scaled version of the same thing (figure 3.5).

The experience shares the same essence: security and anticipation accompany the turn of a corner into the stir of a business district, with the refuge of a neighborhood street just behind. The core of urbane living experiences revolves around some version of this relationship.

The towns of eastern Pennsylvania and Maryland—such as West Chester, Carlisle, Chambersburg, and Frederick—provide that environment with their mixtures of row houses, town houses, and houses on individual yards adjacent to their

Figure 3.1. Gramercy Park West, New York. The streets surrounding the park are quiet and clearly residential.

Figure 3.2. Twentieth Street, New York. The walk east on Twentieth Street toward Third Avenue passes a mixture of institutions and residential buildings.

brick business districts. In the Midwest, such towns as Naperville, Illinois; Marshall Michigan; and Noblesville, Indiana are slightly more spread out. Instead of row houses, they have a mixture of house sizes all on individual lots but with the same sense of adjacency. That midwestern structure for a town extends itself on west from Kearney, Nebraska, to Chico, California, and up into the agricultural centers of Oregon. New England, the Spanish Southwest, and the coastal towns of the Pacific have their own variations. Across the United States, many communities have kept, and

Figure 3.3. Twentieth Street, New York. The approach to Third Avenue gives little hint of the change in street atmosphere until just before the intersection is reached.

Figure 3.4. Third Avenue, New York. Third Avenue's concentration of retail businesses contrasts sharply with the character of the Gramercy Park residential neighborhood.

sometimes amplified, their sense of "town-ness", a sense of urbanity on the small scale.

There are, unfortunately, many hundreds more where urbanity, even on its smallest scale, has been lost. In these places, pleasant in-town neighborhoods are filled with shade trees, interesting old houses, and a mix of people of many age-groups. But these places are no more connected to their centers than are the neighborhoods farther out. They are close in distance, but not connected enough to form a useful union between them and the center; they are like a divorced couple living in

Figure 3.5. Broad Street, Nevada City, California. The approach from a neighborhood into the commercial center of a small town can provide a sense of anticipation and a quickening of pace that are smaller in scale than but still similar to city neighborhoods.

the same house, each continuing with a separate life. A truly successful downtown needs connection. The bulk of business activity may result from folks who drive from out of town or from farther distant neighborhoods within the same town, but the people who live there are essential to an authentic sense of town. Nearly a hundred years ago, John Nolen referred to the need for business districts to be embedded in neighborhoods: "One's home town might mean a good deal more if it were actually a 'home' town."[2]

Writer Richard Lingeman gives a spare description of the importance of residential districts to small-town character: "Most towns were, then, made up of streets of homes—of houses on neat rectangular yards, always one to a family, lining the tree-shaded streets marching out in orderly grid pattern from the business district. To every family a house, and these houses in their collectivity made up the town and gave it its look."[3] The way that the neighborhoods meet the downtown will set the visual, spatial, and social stage for the downtown, or it will be an island separated.

THE ELEMENTS THAT CREATE CONNECTEDNESS

Certain elements are inextricably linked to the expected image of connection around an embedded downtown. These elements include the simple proximity between districts and land uses; concentrations of the most-valued houses; town institutions, such as churches, lodges, and libraries; and streets lined by trees, "their overarching leafy canopy providing pleasant shade."[4] The connecting zone historically mediated the two districts by meshing them—by building up to and building down from the center. It has, unfortunately, often become a third zone inserted between the other two, a zone where the need to park cars has superseded pedestrian concerns.

Connected neighborhoods and town centers have a practical dimension for pedestrians. Pedestrian route quality and, by extension, the quality of the entire street environment—depends on microclimatic comfort, safety and accessibility, provision of prospect and refuge, and the ability to make environmental sense by reflecting the design qualities of both the neighborhood and the business district. Those characteristics result from the physical design of the street corridor itself and from the land use and site design that surround it. Specific design elements will be discussed in detail in chapter 6; some general design considerations for pedestrian routes include the following:

STREET CORRIDOR DESIGN

- Clear separation with walls, landscaping, or both between parking lots and sidewalks
- Clear separation of the pedestrian zone on the sidewalk from the auto zone in the roadway with trees and other landscaping or street elements
- Minimal interruption of the sidewalk with driveways or parking aprons
- A defined right-of-way edge created by building facades near or adjacent to the right-of-way line, well-landscaped yards and gardens, or entry courts and other pedestrian spaces

SURROUNDING LAND USE

- A visually rich mixture of single-family homes and/or compatibly scaled multifamily homes, churches or other institutions, and businesses in adapted residential buildings
- Tree-shaded lawns where houses are set back, or narrow gardens where houses are set closer to the street
- Close proximity between neighborhoods and densely built commercial areas
- Commercial buildings that are modeled on the residential pattern with landscaped yards and buildings set back slightly from the street or that follow the commercial center model of direct frontage on the street

- Consistent building development that is not interrupted by vacant space or parking lots

Measuring the Strength of Connections

These historic patterns might be considered nostalgic if they did not correspond clearly with contemporary ideas about livable and walkable community design. The community design goals of the movements for New Urbanism and for livable communities clearly look to these historic patterns for a design model that values pedestrians and a mix of land uses and experiences.

If the older towns that serve as the models for current community design practice have declined in their own ability to knit together living, working, and shopping within a walkable and visually connected area, then the solution to that decline depends on an ability to measure change from historic to contemporary conditions against an ideal to determine design directions. Will partial restoration of historic configurations improve the image of connection and improve the function of a walkable community?

Proximate neighborhoods and shopping districts represent to health professionals a model for encouraging more healthy lifestyles. The Centers for Disease Control and Prevention recommend that individuals get moderate exercise, such as walking, a minimum of forty minutes a day, three days a week.[5] Recreational walking beginning and ending at one's home is a way to do this without the added time of driving to a recreational area. Even more time-effectiveness can be gained by utilitarian walking: from home to work, home to shopping or other business, home to school, or work to lunch or shopping. Recreational and utilitarian walking that is embedded within a town is facilitated by safe, comfortable, and interesting walking routes that connect sources of pedestrians (mostly neighborhoods) with destinations (business areas, schools, and recreational areas). It follows logically that street corridors pleasant to pedestrians will also be pleasant to drivers and to those people who reside or work along them.

Although not all have been thoroughly field tested, methods exist for estimating geographic areas possessing latent pedestrian demand. The city of Portland, Oregon, uses an index called the Pedestrian Potential Index (PPI) to prioritize areas for investment in pedestrian infrastructure.[6] The index focuses on identifying attractors, such as schools, parks, or neighborhood retail, but does not give weight to the areas that generate pedestrians. Anne Vernez Moudon and her colleagues at the University of Washington have described a method for identifying areas that generate latent demand for pedestrian facilities.[7] These areas have a sufficiently high population density within suitable walking distance of one or more destinations or attractors so that they create a latent demand for walking routes. Moudon's work was specifically targeted at suburban areas and the identification of clusters of higher-density development but is broad enough in concept to be modified for traditional small towns.

Small towns in concept represent an almost ideal situation for daily walking. Pedestrian generators (near-downtown neighborhoods) and a major pedestrian attractor (the commercial and institutional business of the town center) are proximate enough to create pedestrian demand. The older neighborhoods should already have a well-developed pedestrian infrastructure because they were built in a time when walking was considered an important transportation choice for short trips. Many small towns also have neighborhood schools with residential neighborhoods within walking distance.

How do typical small towns or older neighborhoods centered on shopping districts fit the pedestrian supply-and-demand model? A useful concept for evaluating this is the idea of a walkshed. Like a watershed, which is the land area whose surface runoff all flows to a defined point, a walkshed is a land area within a defined walking range of a defined destination. Further research is needed to verify the distances that should be considered "walkable" between residences and activity centers, but walksheds between one quarter mile and one half mile in radius have generally been accepted.[8] The neighborhoods surrounding downtown West Chester, Pennsylvania, exemplify the kinds of places that create pedestrian demand for walking facilities to a destination—in this case the downtown business district. The neighborhoods are compact and consist of single-family homes, row houses, traditional two-family houses, and apartments. West Chester has a population of 17,861, with 6,772 residents within a walkshed extending one quarter mile from the edge of downtown and 12,960 residents one half mile from the edge of downtown[9] (figure 3.6).

With approximately one third of the population within one quarter mile and two thirds within one half mile of the historic commercial district, distance is not a significant barrier to walking between residences and downtown destinations in a town like West Chester. Potential pedestrian demand may exist, and the distances may be reasonable, but realizing the demand also depends on a reasonable walking environment. West Chester's streets and sidewalks intuitively appear to support walking with a safe and comfortable pedestrian environment (figure 3.7).

Intuition and experience are adequate to make a preliminary appraisal of a town like West Chester's pedestrian routes. The ability to consistently evaluate pedestrian environments that connect neighborhoods with commercial centers is important, however, if walking as transportation is to be a goal of town policy makers.[10]

Audit tools have been developed in many North American communities to evaluate pedestrian environments. Audits are conducted by transportation agencies,

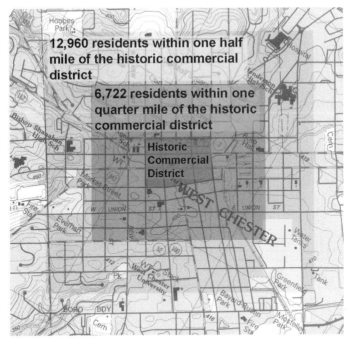

Figure 3.6. West Chester, Pennsylvania. Moderately dense neighborhoods in older towns allow large populations to live within walking distance of commercial districts. Nearly 13,000 people live within a half mile of West Chester, Pennsylvania's central business district.

city governments, and advocacy groups. The Portland Pedestrian Deficiency Index is a streamlined tool that identifies problem areas by considering properties that can be evaluated through geographic information system mapping: missing sidewalks, difficult and dangerous street crossings, and the lack of a connected street network. An audit method developed by Linda Dixon for the City of Gainesville, Florida, is more comprehensive and detailed.[11] The tool allows scoring of individual segments of pedestrian routes based on field observation and measurements of environmental properties. Another audit tool developed by the School of Public Health at the University of North Carolina as part of the Walking and Biking Suitability Audit (WABSA) project is similar.[12] The Dixon and WABSA audit criteria vary only slightly. Combining their areas of overlap and the categories that are unique to each audit results in evaluation criteria for the following conditions:

> *pedestrian facility*: sidewalk continuity, sidewalk width, lack of barriers to accessibility
> *conflicts*: interruptions from driveways and parking aprons, presence or lack of pedestrian signals, signalized control of turn conflicts

Figure 3.7. Gay Street, West Chester, Pennsylvania. Walking routes in West Chester provide strong connections into the downtown district.

> *amenities*: buffer width between walk and curb, lighting, shade trees
> *vehicle level of service*: number of travel lanes, speed limit
> *walk surface*: type, maintenance level.

These criteria, like those used in most audit tools, are weighted heavily toward utilitarian factors, as is appropriate to their use by transportation agencies. Because of that emphasis, they account well for safety but give minimal opportunity to evaluate perceived comfort and aesthetic quality. If all other things were equal, a route segment bordered by an unscreened parking lot would score the same as a route segment along a row of attractive and actively used retail buildings or along a well-landscaped park. Comprehensive evaluations focused on the connections between historic downtowns and their surrounding neighborhoods, however, should consider the aesthetic impact of adjacent land along with utilitarian factors of the path itself.

On-street parking is another element that influences the development of pedestrian space but that is often excluded from walkability audits. Particularly in the transition to a commercial zone, where tree lawns may not exist, parked cars may be the only physical obstruction between pedestrians and moving cars. In that sense, they provide a very real buffer and add to pedestrians' sense of security. Measuring the level of visual and physical connectivity provided by street corridors should be scored with criteria that consider traditional walkability audits, land use considerations, and the presence of parked cars and other buffers between pedestrians and travel lanes.

An audit tool incorporating these criteria was developed and used to rate corridors in the three case studies presented in this chapter (figure 3.8). Use of the tool allows a value to be assigned to each side of each block segment of a street by adding together the scores for each criterion. For example, a side of a block-long street segment with a continuous five-foot walk, no interruptions from driveways, a buffer

Block description

		Point values			
		0	1	2	3
Walkway	Width	> or = 5 feet	3 – 5 feet	< 3 feet	
	Continuity	Continuous	Partial	None	
	Interruptions from driveways and parking aprons	None	Less than 20%	20 – 50%	> 50%
Buffer	Width	> 4 feet	2 – 4 feet	< 2 feet	no buffer
	Street trees	Spacing < 50 feet	Spacing < 100 feet	Spacing > 100 feet	None
	On-street parking lanes	Yes	No		
Street side	Number of travel lanes	2 lanes	2 – 4 lanes	> 4 lanes	
	Speed limit	< or = 25 mph	25 – 35 mph	40 – 45 mph	> 45 mph
Private side	Land use	Buildings on walk or landscaped yards	Effectively screened parking or open lawn	Ineffectively screened parking	Unscreened parking
	Percentage of block length occupied by condition	%	%	%	%
	Multiply point value by percentage of block				
Subtotal each column					
Grand total point value for block					

Figure 3.8. An audit tool used to measure the environmental quality of walking routes connecting residential and business districts should account for physical conditions inside and outside of rights-of-way.

that is five feet wide, with closely spaced street trees, a parallel parking lane, two travel lanes, a twenty-five-mile-per-hour speed limit, and landscaped yards in front of houses would score no points (figure 3.9).

The highest score (22 points) would be assigned to a block segment with no walk, more than 50 percent of the edge consisting of drives and parking aprons, no buffer, no street trees, no parking lane, more than four lanes of traffic, a speed limit greater than forty-five miles per hour, and unscreened parking lots adjacent to the right-of-way (figure 3.10).

Figure 3.9. Jones Street, Savannah, Georgia. A pedestrian walk with characteristics that favor walkability. It would thus have a low score in an audit.

Figure 3.10. Ninth Street, Hopkinsville, Kentucky. A pedestrian walk with characteristics that do not favor walkability. It would thus have a high score in an audit.

THREE CASE STUDIES

Three case studies are presented (1) to explore the change in quality of connections over a long period of time in one community and (2) to profile two other communities' efforts to strengthen connections.

First, the Chevy Chase area of Lexington, Kentucky, is a neighborhood retail district that has seen growth and ineffective site development control steadily erode its sense of connection to its surrounding neighborhoods. The first case description measures the degree of change along its connecting streets from the late 1930s to the present.

Second, West Main Street in Danville, Kentucky, is the link between Centre College and downtown Danville. It is also U.S. Highway 150, and in the 1950s and 1960s its institutional and residential land uses were converted to highway-style strip development. At the same time, the pavement width was expanded at the expense of tree lawns and pedestrian walks. The second case description examines Danville's effort to reconnect college and downtown with pedestrian space improvements in the West Main corridor.

Third, Bardstown Road in Louisville, Kentucky, is a long commercial corridor surrounded by suburban neighborhoods that were built in the highlands to the east of the city in the early twentieth century. The third case description looks at the effect of the site plan controls for new development in Louisville's form districts on the improvement of the pedestrian environment.

Chevy Chase, Lexington, Kentucky

The Chevy Chase shopping area in Lexington, Kentucky, is a commercial center that grew around a streetcar stop. Chevy Chase was on the edge of Lexington until 1919, when Henry Clay's former estate, Ashland, was developed into the Ashland Park neighborhood. The subdivision plan, prepared by the Olmsted Brothers, included a provision for the streetcar line to make a loop through the outer edge of the neighborhood before returning to downtown Lexington.

Several other suburban neighborhoods were developed southwest of Ashland Park over the following decade, and by the mid-1930s development of the large Chevy Chase residential neighborhood was under way. The newly developing shopping area was now surrounded on three sides by residential development that housed a mix of income groups in apartment flats, bungalow-style houses, and a variety of larger, mostly Colonial Revival houses.

By 1950, the Chevy Chase neighborhood was completely developed, and the shopping area was serving about five thousand households with many of their daily services.[13] The shopping area had a focus on daily necessities provided by hardware

Figure 3.11. Lexington, Kentucky. The Chevy Chase shopping district is embedded within a residential district. Commercial buildings are shown in black, parking lots are gray, and residential buildings are white.

stores, pharmacies, groceries, flower shops, dry cleaners, cafés and bars, and gasoline stations.

The population served by the shopping area has remained stable for the past fifty years. It has always been a relatively affluent mix, but with an increasing number of University of Kentucky students in the neighborhoods to its west. The walkshed for the shopping district is relatively concentric, with three main streets that are the pedestrian "arterials" into the district. One of those is Euclid Avenue, leading into the district from the west. Lateral streets feed on to Euclid, and it provides a route into the shopping district that does not cross other major automobile arterials. Because Euclid Avenue is the pedestrian connection with the fewest major obstacles and the best direct connection, its qualitative changes over time are profiled here (figure 3.11).

Physical Characteristics of the Shopping Center at the End of the Streetcar Era

Lexington's streetcar system shut down in 1938. This event symbolized the nearly complete integration of automobiles into daily transportation in Chevy Chase. There were already three gasoline filling stations and two auto repair garages in the small commercial district. Like the sundry other items local residents were able to obtain from area merchants, local residents were able to feed and care for their cars near their neighborhood. The filling stations were of the type that literally filled cars out on the street, however, and parking for these and other businesses had not yet made any serious encroachment off of the streets.

The commercial area was small in 1938. Only 1,080 feet of street frontage was devoted to commercial uses. These businesses were lined up on the irregular line of one side of an irregularly shaped block and the corner of an adjacent block. Neighborhood houses faced the businesses from across the streets or were directly adjacent to the commercial properties. The edge between commercial and residential use was remarkably crisp and matter-of-fact. There was no area that specifically made a transition between the two uses. Three houses were still included within the commercial area, making it something of a blend. These were replaced or false-fronted for commercial use within a decade (figure 3.12).

Chevy Chase has never been a beautiful or quaint shopping area, and that was certainly true in 1938. The commercial buildings were outstandingly undistinguished but served the neighborhood in a sturdy fashion and housed eighteen businesses. The year's business directory indicates that there were five groceries, two

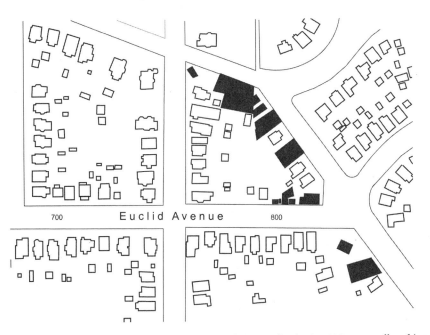

Figure 3.12. Lexington, Kentucky. The Chevy Chase shopping district in 1938 was small and integrated seamlessly with the adjacent neighborhood. Commercial buildings are shown in black, and residential buildings are white.

candy stores, a dry cleaners, a pharmacy, a dairy, an ice company, a liquor store, an unspecified office, the Fleenor Bus Lines storage room, the three filling stations, and the auto repair garage. All of the businesses functioned without off-street parking lots.

Most lots in the surrounding neighborhood were fifty feet wide, with houses typically set back twenty feet from the sidewalk. The houses closest to the commercial area were mostly irregularly shaped cottages with pyramidal roofs of a kind very common in Lexington and typical throughout the Upper South.[14]

The pedestrian infrastructure leading to the shopping area was good. Sidewalks were uninterrupted by driveways and parking aprons. Ample tree lawns with large shade trees separated sidewalks from street curbs. The curb lanes of the streets were reserved for parallel parking. There were no parking lots on properties leading into the commercial district: the residential properties met the sidewalks with lawns, and the commercial buildings fronted directly on the rights-of-way (figure 3.13).

The 600 and 700 blocks of Euclid Avenue were the last two residential blocks leading into the 800 block, where the commercial district began. An audit of the pedestrian route as it existed in 1938 along Euclid Avenue's 600 and 700 blocks would receive a score of 2 on a scale where 0 represents the best possible score and

Figure 3.13. High Street and Euclid Avenue, Lexington, Kentucky. Euclid Avenue in the 1930s had continuous sidewalks separated from the roadway by tree lawns and joined on the other side by residential lawns. In the commercial district, business buildings fronted directly on the walks.

22 represents the worst possible score. The two elements that caused the audit to score points were the four-foot sidewalk width and the average space of greater than 100 feet between street trees.

Contemporary Physical Conditions on Euclid Avenue

Chevy Chase today retains some of its old role as a neighborhood center and has adopted new ones: as a center for specialty shops and as the home to a supermarket, large drugstore, and several bars and restaurants. The most significant physical change is the growth in area devoted to commerce, the addition of parking lots, and the widening of Euclid Avenue's roadway. The total land area devoted to commercial enterprise has grown from two acres to nineteen acres, with buildings and parking lots accounting for about 90 percent of the land outside of the street rights-of-way.

The 800 block of Euclid Avenue is still configured as a traditional commercial street, with ten-foot-wide sidewalks, parallel parking lanes, and buildings directly abutting the right-of-way. The next two blocks—600 and 700—are now largely fronted by parking lots (figure 3.14).

An audit of the pedestrian walks on Euclid Avenue's 600 and 700 blocks as they exist now yields a composite score of 12.5 on a scale where 0 represents the best

Figure 3.14. Lexington, Kentucky. The sidewalks on Euclid Avenue's 600 and 700 blocks today are interrupted by parking lot entrances and are not buffered from the street by parallel parking or a tree lawn.

possible score and 22 represents the worst possible score. This relatively low score results from a narrow sidewalk width of four feet, frequent interruptions by driveways or parking aprons, no buffer space or street trees, no parallel parking on the street, and ineffectively screened or buffered parking lots.

Euclid Avenue, like so many of its counterparts in towns everywhere, has clearly deteriorated as a pedestrian corridor linking neighborhoods to a commercial center. The causes of that deterioration are clear. Reduced pedestrian route quality is a result not of conversion to commercial land use itself but of the specific type of land and building development that resulted from the conversion. The classic strip-style pattern of individual commercial buildings on properties largely devoted to parking is poorly reconciled with the older residential development into which it has been inserted. The street right-of-way is narrow, and available width is devoted to traffic lanes without space for parallel parking lanes or tree lawns. The commercial properties have limited available space because of the size of the residential lots on which they were built. This lack of space and Lexington's standards for development approval have not encouraged developers to provide meaningful landscape buffers or pedestrian space that expands beyond the city's narrow sidewalks. These conditions are endemic to older neighborhood shopping districts and the fringes of small-town centers.

The important question is how to feasibly make pedestrian improvements within the financial and physical constraints of the existing conditions. This case is discussed further after the two remaining case studies. Two nearby commercial districts, downtown Danville and the Highlands district of Louisville, illustrate different approaches to improving pedestrian connections to retail districts. In Danville, the public right-of-way is being improved, and in Louisville, site-planning standards are improving conditions adjacent to the right-of-way.

Danville, Kentucky

West Main Street connects Centre College with the downtown commercial district in Danville, Kentucky. The long two blocks between the college and the retail area were traditionally home to a mix of large houses and institutions, including churches, a lodge, and the library. An early-twentieth-century photograph taken from the steeple of First Presbyterian Church shows the condition of the street corridor that accompanied the residential and institutional land use mix. It wasn't fancy, but board fences, street trees, and a generous walk were bordered by large lawns on one side and by the vehicular way on the other (figure 3.15).

When U.S. Highway 150 was created, it was routed on Main Street through the center of Danville. The blocks between the college and the downtown converted to an

Figure 3.15. Danville, Kentucky. The walks on West Main Street were bordered by mature street trees and residential yards.

auto-oriented commercial strip during the 1950s and 1960s. The highway eventually had four traffic lanes and parallel parking on both sides. Out of the one-hundred-foot-wide right-of-way, seventy-two feet was paved for cars, leaving fourteen feet on each side between the curb face and the property line. The walks were an ample eight feet wide, but unfortunately they were not located at the edge of the right-of-way. This left room for a narrow lawn strip on either side of the walk instead of one wider tree lawn between the walk and the curb. The grass strip was not planted with street trees and in many sections had been paved over so that paved surfaces were unbroken from the fronts of buildings all the way to the curb (figure 3.16).

Danville's city government made a choice to improve the conditions within the right-of-way while accepting the existing conditions on private property. A landscape buffer ordinance could be applied only if substantial changes were being made to properties. Stable property values and land use made it unlikely that demolition and new construction projects subject to a revised development ordinance would be occurring in the near future.

The general strategy was straightforward: reestablish walk continuity and restore tree lawns. Walks were relocated to the outer edges of the right-of-way and were narrowed to a consistent five feet. This allowed for an eight-foot-wide tree lawn to be constructed and planted with street trees (figure 3.17).

An estimated audit score based on the conditions in 1900 is 2.5. This low score is a result of the continuous street trees, buffer width, and residential lawns. The audit score previous to the tree lawn and walk reconstruction was 12; following

Figure 3.16. Danville, Kentucky. Parking lot entries and inadequate buffers caused pedestrian connections to deteriorate on Main Street by the 1990s.

Figure 3.17. Danville, Kentucky. Reconstruction of walks and tree lawns restored stronger pedestrian connections to Main Street in Danville.

reconstruction, it is 5 out of a possible range from 0 to 22. The audit score could be improved if parking areas were more adequately screened.

The Highlands, Louisville, Kentucky

The Highlands neighborhood developed in the early twentieth century south of Cherokee Park, Frederick Law Olmsted's great masterwork of park design. It has remained one of Louisville's most pleasant and desirable residential areas and over the years has been served by the linear commercial district on Baxter Boulevard and Bardstown Road. The mix of eclectic shops, restaurants, bars, and professional services draws clientele from well beyond the neighborhood. Bardstown Road is thriving, interesting, and congested, and it has a variety of property types. Earlier, houses were converted to or replaced by small-scale commercial buildings that abutted the sidewalk edge (figure 3.18). Later, in some sections of Bardstown Road, buildings were replaced with fast-food restaurants and other parking-dominated businesses. These segments began to lose the elements that gave them visual cohesiveness: a fairly consistent scale of street enclosure, and a tight interval in the spacing of the storefronts (figure 3.19).

Louisville adopted a new land development code in 2003 that included development regulations for a variety of form districts. The form districts concept recognized that different types of neighborhoods and precincts had site-planning and building traditions that were essential to their character. Zoning alone could not ensure that the character of these districts would be maintained or strengthened. Bardstown Road is part of a "Traditional Marketplace Corridor" form district. The Traditional Marketplace Corridors are "characterized by older, pedestrian-scale development along major roadways adjacent to traditional neighborhoods."[15] The

Figure 3.18. Louisville, Kentucky. Bardstown Road was already a thriving linear commercial district in the 1920s.

Figure 3.19. Louisville, Kentucky. The Bardstown Road corridor is nearly chaotic in places, but its strongest characteristic is still the intimate scale of smaller buildings creating a varied but contained street edge.

standards for the corridors essentially provide for new buildings to be built adjacent to and facing the right-of-way, for parking to be behind or to the side of buildings, for curb cuts to be minimized, and for the design of the pedestrian walk to be well considered.

Several new buildings have been constructed on Baxter Avenue and Bardstown Road since the form district standards have been in effect. Two recently built buildings illustrate the positive impact that the thoughtful development of individual properties can have on street corridors and pedestrian ways. The collective potential of incremental change is great in an area like the Highlands, where property redevelopment happens with greater frequency because of the higher potential rewards for investment.

The building at 955 Baxter Avenue is a mixed-use project built to emulate the commercial buildings developed on Baxter Avenue and Bardstown Road in the early twentieth century. It is three stories, brick, with prominent display windows and a courtyard in front of the recessed middle section of the building. It was set back ten feet from the original sidewalk edge so that the sidewalk could be widened (figure 3.20).

The Taco Bell building on Bardstown Road is an unequivocal representation of contemporary fast-food chain architecture. It has, however, one important

Figure 3.20. Louisville, Kentucky. The building at 955 Baxter Avenue creates a simple but adequate pedestrian space and has room for café tables.

distinction from the majority of its commercial siblings: it is built on the street line with minimal interruption of the pedestrian walk. The pedestrian entrance to the building actually faces the sidewalk, with steps leading down to sidewalk level. The walk crosses a twenty-four-foot-wide entrance drive on one side of the building and a twelve-foot-wide drive-through exit lane on the other side of the building. While these are still interruptions in the walk, they are minimal indeed for a drive-in restaurant (figure 3.21).

Neither of these buildings is extravagant in its design; in fact, both are typical of their types. But they have been well sited and have responded to the scale of the neighborhood and their own adjacency to a pedestrian walk. An audit of the walk segment in front of each property yields a score of 3 for 955 Baxter Avenue and a score of 8 for the Taco Bell property. A property two blocks east that is typical of those that were developed before the form district was enacted was audited for comparison and received a score of 12 points (figure 3.22).

Danville and Louisville's Highlands neighborhood represent two halves of a comprehensive strategy: setting reasonable land development standards and rehabilitating street infrastructure to more adequately accommodate pedestrians. In an ideal world, both halves would be implemented at the same time. Reality does, however, interfere. In the case of a town like Danville, development standards may create

Figure 3.21. Bardstown Road, Louisville, Kentucky. Taco Bell's building follows the corporate standard, but its site plan also accommodates pedestrians.

Figure 3.22. Louisville, Kentucky. Construction on Bardstown Road before the form district guidelines were enacted generally eroded street character.

very little improvement in the near term because the pace of property redevelopment is slow. Standards are certainly appropriate, but they should not be expected to have any real effect on the ground for a long time. In that case, rehabilitating the public infrastructure to improve neighborhood-downtown pedestrian connections will create greater improvement more quickly.

The Highlands neighborhood represents the converse situation. The public right-of-way is narrow and choked with auto travel lanes, parallel parking, and the sidewalk. The spatial structure within the right-of-way would be changed with difficulty, though improvements could be made to walk surfaces, pedestrian signals, and accessibility barriers. Improving the spatial structure of the corridor largely depends on the nature of development on the edge of the street. Because the business district is thriving and in constant flux, development standards have great potential to transform Baxter Avenue and Bardstown Road in ways that are much more sensitive to the comfort and pleasure of pedestrians. That transformation has, in fact, already begun.

To return to Euclid Avenue in Chevy Chase: it represents the effect of priorities and the history of where we place them. The transportation priority on Euclid Avenue in the early part of the twentieth century was balanced between pedestrians and automobiles. The design of the avenue reflected that balance with an adequate tree lawn buffer between the walk and the travel lanes, with street trees, with on-street parking, and without parking lot or driveway entrances cutting across the pedestrian sidewalk. Later, the priority shifted to automobiles. The tree lawns and the parking lanes were sacrificed for additional travel lanes. Drives and parking lot entrances cut across the sidewalks, and the yards of residential properties were converted to parking lots.

Laypeople—nondesigners and nonplanners—are not insensitive to environmental quality. They know when a street corridor is unwelcoming and uncomfortable, and they will avoid these corridors. Conversely, if there is a destination and there is a source of pedestrians, they will use a corridor whose design priority corresponds with their needs. Designing street corridors with a priority on pedestrians will create general visual enhancement of streets by providing detail, variety, and layering that will also appeal to drivers. This balanced approach returns corridors to something more like the ideal environmental images represented in historic photographs and memories of the streets that connect neighborhoods and commercial centers.

CHAPTER FOUR

Walking Downtown:
The Visitor's Experience

Chapter 3 described the issues of connection between commercial centers and the residential areas around them. Because there are so many other retail options available to the people within a center's walkshed, however, it is clear that a downtown should not expect to survive economically based on the walking market alone. As they always have, downtowns must provide opportunities for people from other towns or more distant parts of their own towns to visit and do business. These people will most likely arrive by automobile, park, and then walk on to one or more destinations. This chapter considers the circulation experiences of those visitors and documents the qualities of common pedestrian routes found in commercial districts.

I have used my own community of Winchester, Kentucky, to illustrate the design issues of the downtown pedestrian experience. Winchester is a town of 15,000 residents located twenty miles from Lexington, a city of 275,000. Winchester's downtown has a large stock of mostly intact late-nineteenth-century commercial buildings. Business is not quite booming in the downtown, but along with the law offices and the gift and antique shops, you can shop at a drugstore, a grocery, and a hardware store. You can eat a good breakfast, lunch, or dinner; visit the library; or buy shoes, clothes, pets, flowers, or furniture.

I go downtown often, though I cannot do all of my shopping there. As a resident and a frequent visitor, I have discovered repeated patterns of experience that I would have disregarded if looking at the district with only a designer's eyes. When walking or driving downtown, my experience unites a set of separate paths into a circulation pattern. Many different circulation patterns are created downtown, and each one is shared by many people. For most people, these patterns combine movement by car and by foot.

Each circulation pattern is a continuum that converts auto drivers to pedestrians and then back again. The point of conversion from driver to pedestrian is a significant change in the experience. From that point, there is a greater awareness of movement through space, and the experience of circulation becomes a path through a sequence of spaces shared with cars.

In his book *Design of Cities*, Edmund Bacon emphasized the linkage between movement and spatial experience in towns and cities. He believed that "the points of connection between systems should be places of special emphasis and design enrichment."[1] One of these points of connection is the "moment of transfer from a vehicle to the ground, and movement on foot to one or another destination in the city."[2] Bacon wrote about cities, but movement directs spatial experience in smaller centers as well. What kinds of experiences are created by arrival sequences in small downtowns? How do they compare with the experience of the shopping centers that compete with them for commercial and social activity?

Using a series of photographs, circulation sequences in Winchester were documented that represent the types of pedestrian routes found in many towns. The sequences were then evaluated in two ways: (1) with the objective criteria used to plan shopping centers and (2) with the more qualitative criteria of urban design practice. The method described could easily be used in other towns to evaluate the quality of pedestrian experience, to analyze the need for improvements, and to guide the location of future parking development.

PEDESTRIAN MOVEMENT IN SHOPPING CENTERS

Shopping centers compete directly with the retail and service businesses of downtowns. Much of their success derives from the symbiotic evolution of their spatial organization and the increasing dominance of automobile transportation through the twentieth century. Since the first Sears stores in suburban locations opened in the 1920s in Memphis, Los Angeles, and other cities in the United States, shopping center developers and designers have considered circulation a primary design issue.[3] The idea of managing circulation for efficiency was so important in the early period of shopping center development that some large shopping centers were built with traffic control towers manned by a parking space spotter. The spotter was equipped with switches to control traffic lights at the ends of the aisles to indicate available spaces.[4]

The fifties were an experimental period for shopping center design, and several circulation and parking models were considered appropriate to differing site conditions. The main differences between models involved parking location—in front of the stores, behind the stores, or split between the front and the back. Parking in the front emulated the ideal downtown situation where one could park at the curb in front of a business—but with many more parking spaces than had traditionally been available and with businesses fronting only one side of the parking area. Parking spaces in the back were found to cause conflicts with service entrances and created a need for arcades to penetrate through to the front of the buildings.[5] The rear parking formula had evolved into the enclosed shopping mall by the 1970s. Lateral distance and screening were used to separate service entrances and pedestrian entrances.

One refined and proven formula remained for unenclosed shopping centers: service in the rear, parking in the front, an access lane along the storefronts, and an encircling lane around the parking area. In this concept, the pedestrian is provided a simple circulation experience. The governing idea is that pedestrians should be able to get into the shops easily. They should be inside purchasing products rather than outside enjoying the architecture. The design of the building facade and its position in the site plan are critical.

The design criteria for pedestrian movement in shopping center site plans became explicit by the mid-1960s.[6] First, facades and signs should be visible when shoppers begin walking. Second, shoppers should be able to walk up parking aisles to the building without having to go between parked cars. Next, service areas and activities should be separated from pedestrian areas, and finally, shoppers should not have to walk more than 300 feet, ideally, and 450 feet as an absolute maximum.[7]

Shopping centers have strongly and simply combined the experiences of driving, walking, and shopping. No other commercial organization matches the brevity, immediacy, and clarity of their arrival sequences. Shopping center site planning has been codified in practice and has formed the shopping experience of three generations of shoppers. Traditional urban commercial districts are now compared against a solidified set of experiential expectations based on the convenience of shopping centers. This is important to consider in downtowns because of their continuing competition with shopping centers. Whereas downtowns offer such advantages as ambience and a more diverse mix of professional and governmental services to go with retail, access is still perceived to be more convenient in shopping centers. Downtowns should not become like shopping centers—this would destroy most of what makes them distinctive, and they would lose the advantages of mixed land use—but they should strive for greater clarity in their internal pedestrian circulation patterns.

PEDESTRIAN MOVEMENT IN DOWNTOWNS

Facilitating movement has also been an issue throughout the history of American downtowns. The capacity of downtown buildings to sell merchandise or to carry out public and private business has never been seriously questioned, but the ability of the circulation matrix to deliver people comfortably to those buildings has always been in question. Through the late nineteenth century, the needs were basic. There was mud: "In winter, Main Street was a series of frozen gorges and hummocks; in fall and spring, a river of mud; in summer, a continuing dust heap; it was the best street in Plattville."[8] Foot traffic had to be kept away from it, and horse-drawn traffic had to be prevented from sinking into it.

At the close of the nineteenth century, functional improvements to drainage and waste removal had been made, but the dirt, disorganization, and continuing rawness created a need to civilize the street environment. The civic improvement movement in many towns paved streets with brick and provided decent walks, street lighting, and street trees where possible.

Modern road engineering developed in the 1920s. Streets were better constructed and drained, and cars were common. For a time, there was a lively coexistence between cars and people in small downtowns. In many towns, including Winchester, cars were parked perpendicular to traffic down the center of the street. Traffic engineering caught up with road engineering by the forties, and emphasis shifted from *parking* cars to *moving* cars on downtown streets. The emphasis on movement, combined with the continuing need to park cars, created demand for off-street parking lots. Cars' needs began to supersede those of pedestrians. Many of the humanizing elements advocated by the civic improvement movement, such as trees and pedestrian-scaled street lamps, were removed to devote more surface to automobiles.

Irreversible change came after World War II, when the competition with shopping centers seriously threatened downtowns. At first, older business districts competed by copying the architectural features of the shopping centers. This failed to halt decline, however, because it neglected the issue of access; the end result was the destruction of detail-rich building facades by making them into poor imitations of strip center buildings. Because they could not duplicate the simplified parking arrangement of shopping centers, many towns began in the 1960s and 1970s to differentiate their traditional commercial centers with pedestrian-focused plans. Short of creating complete pedestrian precincts, pedestrians have been accommodated with thematic walk lighting, street trees, building facade rehabilitation, and detailed walk paving.

The design theories that established the basis for landscape redevelopment in small downtowns were outlined in the 1960s in such books as Kevin Lynch's *Image of the City* and Gordon Cullen's *Townscape*. The principles they articulated are still considered valid by most urban designers. The criteria for design of pedestrian routes can be distilled into five elements:

- Pathways should possess continuity of design quality.[9]
- Landmarks or intermediate destinations should define path segments to enhance legibility.[10]
- Paths should present visual variety or complexity to reduce perception of long distances.[11]
- Paths should provide a sense of prospect and refuge that comes from well-developed pathway edges.
- Paths should be accessible to people with a variety of mobility levels.

PEDESTRIAN ENVIRONMENT IN WINCHESTER

As stated earlier, shopping center convenience standards have created expectations for downtowns even though they present entirely different circumstances. Shopping centers evolved with the car; with less rigidly defined infrastructure, they will easily continue to evolve as long as cars are a primary transportation method. Small downtowns have been in a fifty-year struggle to retrofit themselves for a circulation pattern that incorporates large numbers of moving and parked cars. The dense architectural configuration that is their greatest environmental asset also rigidly limits the ways circulation can be enhanced.

To find out how a small town like Winchester can systematically assess its intra-downtown pedestrian routes, representative parking and walking sequences were identified by making many approaches to downtown using various beginning and destination points. After deliberately moving through the representative sequences several times to understand their characteristic features, the sequences were photographed. The photographs were paced to reveal the sequences as serial experiences. Gordon Cullen, in *Townscape*, described serial experience as a "sequence of revelations"[12] that occurs in the three-dimensional experience of a town. In the sequences photographed in Winchester, the pictures were taken at points where a corner turns, where the path space widens or narrows, or where particular features become prominent.

Winchester's Parking and Pedestrian Route Patterns

Downtown Winchester offers three types of parking-walking-destination scenarios. Because various commercial destinations are similarly situated on or near Main Street, the location of parking governs the nature of the paths. There are three main parking options if one wants to drive and then shop on Main Street.

First, Main Street itself has free two-hour parking for about 150 cars in a three-and-one-half-block stretch. This is all provided as parallel parking on both sides of the street. Second, the first blocks on the streets perpendicular to Main Street and the streets around the courthouse square include another 160 spaces. These spaces are all within 450 feet of Main Street. The third parking option includes about 55 spaces in a municipal parking lot where a person can park legally. There are several business parking lots that people customarily use to park illegally in order to walk over to Main Street. These lots are all found on the back sides of the blocks adjacent to Main Street.

The simplest pedestrian sequence is to park on Main Street close to the destination business, leave the car, and walk on the Main Street sidewalks. The second most desirable sequence is to park on one of the streets perpendicular to Main Street and walk down to Main and then to the business. The third option is to park in one of the parking lots on the other side of the alleys running behind the Main Street business blocks. Because there are no pedestrian connections to Main Street through the buildings, people must walk down an alley or parking aisle to a cross street and then over to Main Street.

An example sequence was selected and evaluated for each of the three patterns. Each example was scrutinized from two perspectives: the criteria for shopping center planning and the criteria generally accepted for urban design.

Sequence 1: Parallel Parking on Main Street

Each sequence involves a series of photographs that successively shows the experience that pedestrians would have after leaving their parked cars. In the first frame of this sequence, two-hour parking spaces are seen lining both sides of Main Street. Experience has shown that these are frequently available. At the moment of arrival and on leaving the car, commercial buildings and signs are clearly visible (figure 4.1).

If one is able-bodied, the steps to the "high side" walk are easily mounted. If, however, a person is pushing a stroller, uses a wheelchair, or has physical difficulty with steps, then a walk along the edge of the street to reach an access ramp is required (figure 4.2).

Figure 4.1. Winchester, Kentucky. On-street parking on Main Street is surrounded by commercial buildings, signs, and activity.

Figure 4.2. Winchester, Kentucky. Main Street's high side has steps that can be difficult to mount.

Figure 4.3. Main Street, Winchester, Kentucky. The high side provides a balanced combination of prospect and refuge.

On the sidewalk at the top of the steps, the view fully encompasses the street space, including building facades, signs, and the street trees that are on the west side of the street. The steps provide an effective layer of separation between auto and pedestrian traffic (figure 4.3).

Shopping Center Criteria for Sequence 1

The first sequence shows that this type of pattern holds up well against the criteria developed for shopping center circulation. Business signs are completely visible at all times. Access to establishments is good. People move from parallel-parked cars immediately onto the sidewalk or steps—although the steps may be difficult for some people to negotiate. Service areas for the shops are located at the rear of the buildings and do not intrude upon the path. Finally, the parking distance is very short; the parking spaces equal the convenience of parking in the fire lane of a shopping center.

Urban Design Character of Sequence 1

This sequence occurs within a single space. The space of the street is well defined by the two- to four-story buildings that line both sides of it. Path continuity is complete within blocks but breaks significantly at intersections.

Intermediate destinations and landmarks are present. The courthouse clock tower and the recess in the street line at the courthouse, in particular, provide an orienting landmark that aids legibility.

The varied building facades and landscape elements offer visual variety, reducing the perception of longer distances. The steps, railings, and shrubs provide varying levels of separation between the pedestrian space and the traffic lanes on the east side of Main Street. On the west side, streetlamps, street trees, and parked cars perform the same function at a lower level. A sense of prospect and refuge is present, particularly on the higher-level walk on the east side.

Mobility is clearly limited by the steps onto the high side walk. On the west side of the street, curb ramps and crosswalks aid mobility.

Sequence 2: Wall Street (Back Side of Courthouse Square) to Main Street

In this sequence, a person would park the car on a side street, such as Wall Street, and then walk to a business on Main Street. After the person parks the car, the view to the left looks across the courthouse lawn to the old post office, which is now used as a courthouse annex (figure 4.4).

Figure 4.4. Wall Street, Winchester, Kentucky. The square has a pleasant balance of public buildings and landscaped lawns as well as abundant diagonal parking spaces.

Figure 4.5. Court Street, Winchester, Kentucky. The shaded walks on the square have clear views of the business buildings on Main Street.

The Court Street walk is bordered by parking on the right and by trees and the courthouse on the left. There is a clear view of the high side of Main Street (figure 4.5). At the corner looking right, the Main Street commercial buildings have a strong presence. There is no light, but crosswalks lead across Main and Court Streets (figure 4.6). At the corner looking left, the walk leads past the courthouse entrance and to the commercial buildings that line North Main Street (figure 4.7).

A crosswalk leads across Main Street to the high side walk, with an accessible ramp shown to the right. Building facades are clearly visible while crossing (figure 4.8). Looking to the right after crossing Main Street, the downtown building and street assemblage is viewed clearly (figure 4.9). The view from the buildings on the east side of Main Street looks back to Wall Street and City Hall (figure 4.10).

Shopping Center Criteria for Sequence 2

The second sequence also holds up well against the criteria developed for shopping center circulation. Business signs on Court and Main Streets are visible to pedestrians at the beginning of the walk. People move from parking spaces immediately onto the sidewalk. Service areas for the shops are located at the rear of the buildings and do not intrude on the path. The parking distance on the square is a maximum of 220 feet from Main Street.

Figures 4.6, 4,7, and 4.8. Winchester, Kentucky. At the intersection of Court and Main, the directional choices—left, right, or straight across the street to the high side—are clearly apparent.

Figure 4.9. Main Street, Winchester, Kentucky. The high side provides clear views and a feeling of separation from traffic.

Figure 4.10. Winchester, Kentucky. The view back down Court Street provides a sense of connection with the beginning point of the path.

Urban Design Character of Sequence 2

The street space around the courthouse is well defined by the facades of buildings on three sides and by the courthouse lawn on the fourth side. Longer-distance views that terminate in parking lots or at the backs of buildings are minimal; most views are of the building fronts that define the immediate street space. Path continuity breaks only to cross Court and Main Streets but maintains strong visual continuity.

The walk up Court Street is shaded and has open views of the facades on Court Street. There is a clear sense of the space ending at the Main Street high side. Legibility is strong in this sequence because the courthouse is the major downtown landmark and the path leads to the high side, a linear landmark.

The view of Main Street buildings becomes wider as pedestrians progress up the walk. Visual variety and complexity are present in a progressive sequence from the parklike setting of the square to the commercial facades of Main Street

Prospect and refuge are provided by the tree canopies and the varied surfaces of the building facades on the streets around the court square. On both sides of Main Street, streetlamps, street trees, and parked cars provide a protective edge, and the sense of prospect and refuge is even stronger on the high side walk.

The height of the walk on the east side of Main Street poses an access challenge, but ramps up to the walk aid mobility.

Sequence 3: Winchester Municipal Parking Lot to Main Street

The third sequence shows how pedestrians would get to Main Street from parking lots behind the Main Street buildings. This particular example begins in the municipal parking lot. As drivers turn from Broadway into the parking area, there is a view of a metal building on the right, sheds on the left, and a barn straight ahead. The parking is in a double-loaded aisle (figure 4.11).

Figure 4.11. Winchester, Kentucky. The view from a car entering the municipal parking lot terminates on a metal barn.

Figure 4.12. Winchester, Kentucky. The driving aisle does double duty as the walkway out of the parking area.

Figure 4.13. Winchester, Kentucky. Building facades on Broadway reflect a low level of commercial activity on the street.

After parking, pedestrians walk down the parking aisle toward Broadway, with a view of a one-story retail building (figure 4.12). As they turn right on the sidewalk leading to Main Street, the view is defined by the building facades of low-intensity commercial space on Broadway (figure 4.13). As the path approaches the intersection with Main Street, the effective sidewalk width is narrowed by trash containers and fire escapes (figure 4.14).

Figure 4.14. Broadway, Winchester, Kentucky. Trash containers, parking meter posts, and a restaurant grease trap clutter a sidewalk that would otherwise be plenty wide.

Upon arrival at Main Street, pedestrians have the choice to turn left or right. The view down Main includes the higher-intensity commercial space on the first floor of two- to four-story buildings, a wide sidewalk, a few trees, a café's barbecue grill, and ornamental light fixtures (figure 4.15).

Shopping Center Criteria for Sequence 3

Sequence 3 falls short of the optimum criteria for shopping centers. A few business signs, for example, become visible in figure 4.14. Wide visibility of signs is not possible until the pedestrian reaches Main Street, shown in the last photograph of the sequence (figure 4.15). The pedestrian path out of the parking lot is in the aisle, which is considered acceptable in shopping centers. Service areas intrude on to the sidewalk, which is not considered acceptable in a shopping center. Parking distance varies from 300 feet to 550 feet away from Main Street. These distances are considered unacceptable in a shopping center.

Urban Design Character of Sequence 3

The path travels through three significantly different spaces: the parking lot, East Broadway, and Main Street. There are no repeated design elements, such as light fixtures, paving materials, or other features, to extend continuity across the three

Figure 4.15. Winchester, Kentucky. Main Street's sidewalk contrasts positively with the earlier segments of the route.

different spaces. The parking lot has no pedestrian improvements, landscaping, pedestrian-scale lighting, or business facades that face on to it. Broadway is a wide, unshaded street whose edges are not enlivened by active business facades. The pedestrian walks are narrow in proportion to the width of the street, giving a sense that they are unimportant. In total, path continuity is relatively weak.

No significant landmarks are visible along the path, and business signs are noticeably absent in the view until Main Street is reached. Legibility is relatively weak as a result.

Visual richness is lacking in the parking area and on Broadway. Visual variety is potentially present in the varied building facades adjacent to the path on Broadway, but poor maintenance, lack of color, and clutter from air conditioners and other utility fixtures prevent its realization.

A partial sense of refuge is provided by parked cars on Broadway, but other elements that would partially define the pedestrian space are lacking in the parking lot and on Broadway. Views are open, giving a good sense of prospect.

The path is accessible through the parking lot and along Broadway. At Main Street, the sidewalks are also accessible, with the exception of the east side of Main turning left from Broadway. In that direction, the high side steps present the same obstacles that they do for the other two routes.

Improving Pedestrian Paths

The three sequences vary in their satisfaction of both sets of criteria. The sequences that began at parking spaces on Main Street or on the square meet the criteria for shopping center development and include strong urban design qualities. For the parking spaces farther from Main Street, the sequence deteriorates. According to shopping center criteria, the major problems with the paths originating away from Main Street are the mixing of service areas with pedestrian paths and the inability to see one's destination for much of the walk. From an urban design standpoint, the qualities that make Main Street so positive—path continuity, visual variety, and a series of destinations—are mostly lacking from the lateral streets, parking areas, and connecting alleyways.

It doesn't have to be this way. Walking distances for most of the parking spaces downtown are within the criteria for shopping centers. For the ones that are too far, possibilities exist for creating new pedestrian routes that lead more directly to Main Street. Removing conflicts with service functions is a shared responsibility of the public and private property owners, but it can be done.

Creating ways to see a Main Street destination from all points of the pedestrian routes is not possible, so this goal will never be fully met. It is possible to mitigate the situation, however, by extending business signage, the attention to building detail, and the landscape elements from Main Street onto the lateral streets. Such treatment would enhance the visual connection between the parking areas and business destinations.

The elements necessary for a high level of urban design quality are also present in downtown Winchester. A set of landmarks or intermediate destinations is in place, and development of views to them could incorporate them into pedestrian routes. Path continuity can be created by working with the existing fabric along pedestrian routes. Developing greater visual variety rests largely with building owners and shopkeepers. The design and maintenance of their properties control the subject matter of the visual environment downtown.

Good pedestrian experiences have a sense of being somewhere and of moving toward something. For all their supposed nothingness, better shopping centers possess a strong two-dimensional graphic identity that provides for a sense of moving to something.

That same sense, but in a robust three-dimensional version, makes the walk from Winchester's courthouse square to Main Street surpass simple convenience. Pedestrians are in a comfortably identifiable space moving toward a graphically appealing destination. In Winchester and many other towns, financial and organizational systems are being modified in ways that renew downtown commercial development. An indicator of continuing success will be more people downtown. They will use the existing patterns of circulation and will create new patterns. The neglected edges of the center will achieve new prominence as points of change from the automobile to foot travel. More people will experience the paths from the edges. The landscape will evolve to serve the patterns of use that result from a growing economy, or it will be a limiting factor in the life of the downtown.

If the general principles of efficient shopping center planning and good urban design are applied to experiential assessment of downtown pathways, then real problems and opportunities can be identified. The design and construction that result will be better and more useful if they contribute to the sense of being somewhere and of moving toward something.

Chapter 5 will discuss parking organization as the key link between auto and pedestrian circulation in greater detail. This discussion will focus on three aspects of parking: its role in creating pedestrian routes, the impact that it has on the built fabric of commercial centers, and the balance that must be created between convenience for visitors who drive and walkable linkages for those who live in neighborhoods near commercial centers.

The Arrangement of Parking: A Design Perspective

CHAPTER FIVE

Chapter 4 discussed the role that parking location—as the beginning point for many pedestrian trips—plays in determining pedestrian experience. This chapter focuses specifically on parking arrangement and the relationships between parking and other elements of downtown fabric.

Various design and planning approaches have been used in the United States since the late 1950s to adapt older town centers to contemporary circulation and parking needs. Complete street or precinct pedestrianization plans based on the models of Victor Gruen and executed most prominently by Lawrence Halprin and Garrett Eckbo were attempted in many towns.[1] However, they were found to work only in a few special circumstances.[2] In diluted versions of the early pedestrianization schemes, downtown revitalization plans funded by Urban Development Action Grants and other sources, and inspired by Gorden Cullen's book *The Concise Townscape*, emphasized materials, furnishings, and plantings to diminish the effect of auto circulation on pedestrians.[3] These plans typically focused on only one or a few specific streets and were not necessarily preservation oriented. A more comprehensive extension of the main street revitalization plan is the corridor planning concept that identifies one or more important street corridors leading to downtown. These corridors are redesigned according to the varying land use conditions and circulation characteristics along their length.[4]

Despite forty years of downtown revitalization design across the United States, parking—and the pedestrian circulation that connects with it—is still a poorly resolved component in most historic downtowns. Downtown parking is often placed ad hoc, with too many different locations and without clear connection to downtown destinations. In many towns with a perceived shortage of parking, parking studies have shown that an appropriate quantity does exist but that those who need the parking cannot find it.[5]

This lack of organization results from treating parking as a single element rather than as a component in a pattern of access. Parking and pedestrian movement are typically considered separately rather than as linked elements. When parking is not considered as a spatial design component, it can become a destructive element in the urban fabric, interrupting the building pattern, separating the commercial center from residential areas, and creating unpleasant pedestrian paths.

Some historic commercial districts do have systems of access that function for the entire sequence of experience. In these towns, parking is accessible and conveniently located, the walking experience is a cohesive spatial sequence, and the historic building pattern is intact. These downtowns do not share similar forms or use the same model for parking and circulation. Their common characteristic is compatibility between their built form and their patterns of circulation. Prescott, Arizona, is such a place.

INTEGRATED ACCESS: PRESCOTT, ARIZONA

Prescott, Arizona, is an unpretentiously great small town. As drivers enter the town center from either direction on Arizona 89, the downtown is at the bottom of a gentle slope. The view from the top is of the large, elm-shaded courthouse square surrounded by commercial blocks. A few strip-style business locations occupy the edge of the downtown, but this is not a barren zone of parking lots or underutilized space.

As drivers approach the square, they begin looking for parking places. Chances are good that one of the diagonal parking places on both sides of the streets encircling the square will be available. If not, the rest of the downtown offers abundant on-street parking as well as three other reservoirs of public parking. Union Street has been converted to three rows of diagonal parking. A driver who leaves a car there can walk directly onto the square and the commercial streets surrounding it. Following a directional sign to the Montezuma Street parking lot allows one to walk out of the lot and be at the prime downtown corner, across from the square, in less than two hundred feet. A third choice is to park in the Granite Street lot, where a large sign directs one into an alleyway leading through the interior of a commercial building. The alleyway is lined with shops, and the exit faces the town square.

Of the four blocks bordering the square, three have no gaps in the line of building facades (figure 5.1). Parking has not intruded into the building pattern. Every storefront is occupied, just as in the rest of the downtown. Visitors to Prescott will inevitably walk into the square and realize that it is the downtown's heart—but with a tree canopy that makes it a place apart from the streets. The square feels so pleasant that in an hour one would be likely to see the same elderly men in cowboy hats, college students reading and talking, and children playing who were seen the first time through (figures 5.2–5.4).

Figure 5.1. Prescott, Arizona. Downtown Prescott is centered on the courthouse square. The building pattern in the commercial blocks around the square is uninterrupted and contributes to an optimal visual and pedestrian environment, yet parking is conveniently close.

Figures 5.2, 5.3, and 5.4. Prescott, Arizona. A typical parking and walking sequence in Prescott covers a short distance before reaching the square and passes through high-quality pedestrian space.

Prescott physically manifests a downtown that is working for the people who use it: an image of the downtown is readily established by visitors; commercial space is fully used, and the building fabric is intact; parking is abundant and easy to use; pedestrian routes are pleasant, direct, and lead to landmarks or imageable places; and people linger in this humane environment.

Prescott clearly owes its success as a place to more than a functioning pattern of access. Many components contribute. Influxes of retirees and college students have boosted the retail economy. Contemporary citizens of Prescott have inherited and conserved a lively and cohesive built environment. New businesses have been established, and the owners of existing stores have been responsive to their market. The town contains a significant public space. Nevertheless, the arrangement of physical access plays an integral role in allowing the other components of the downtown environment to thrive. With a surcharged downtown market, Prescott has managed to satisfy a high demand for parking spaces without destroying its historic fabric.

Towns like Prescott elicit some important questions about the physical retrofitting of historic downtowns for effectively integrating parking that meets contemporary expectations.

- Are there models for organizing access that can provide well-integrated parking and pedestrian connection patterns while retaining the historic resources of downtowns?
- What are the design and preservation characteristics and impacts of different patterns?

This chapter answers these questions with observations made in a group of towns that have economically successful downtowns with significant historic building patterns. The subject towns are distributed regionally across much of the United States but were not chosen to statistically represent particular regional characteristics.

The observed towns represent a particular economic niche: they are in the range of ten thousand to thirty thousand in population, and they have economically successful downtowns that partially depend on tourism, college students, or other markets beyond the local population. They are distinguished not by historic monuments but by an ensemble of older buildings that constitute a traditional downtown form of common-wall buildings without street setbacks. These building ensembles play a prominent role in each town's tourism and marketing efforts. Because of their economic success and their larger market area, they all have significant pressure for parking places. None of the towns have extraordinary financial resources that would preclude them from being a model for parking and access design in similarly sized towns.

Aerial photographs of the towns were used to develop a preliminary sense of town form, circulation, and parking distribution. Base maps were then developed for towns that appeared to possess more distinct patterns of access and parking so that they could be studied in greater detail. All thirty-two towns were field surveyed, and maps were developed for ten of them. Written observations and unscaled diagrams recorded the distribution of building uses, on- and off-street public parking locations and quantities, and pedestrian routes. Scaled mapping and detailed documentation of those observations were made in the ten towns for which base maps had been created.

Documentation included parking quantity and location, pedestrian paths from parking to downtown destinations, photographs of the pedestrian route experience, and the spatial and land use conditions of the street corridors that form the connections between the downtowns and the neighborhoods around them. The notes made in the other towns were used to establish that observed access patterns were not anomalies and also that no distinct patterns were left undescribed. Detailed maps were prepared for the five towns that were the clearest examples of types after the site visits were complete. The study was descriptive and not statistical in nature. The frequent occurrence of particular models was not considered significant because of the impressionistic means by which towns were selected for the study.

The above information was evaluated in two stages. First, done largely in the field, was to categorize types of access patterns. Second, based on notes, maps, and photographs, was to evaluate space and experience in representative towns of each type. Specific comparisons between towns/types were made on the compatibility of the pattern with building preservation (Sanborn fire insurance maps were used to determine what had formerly occupied the sites of off-street parking areas in the mapped towns), the quality of pedestrian experiences, and the maintenance of traditional connections between downtown and surrounding neighborhoods.

PARKING ORGANIZATION AND ACCESS MODELS

Chapter 4 discussed downtown access as a process that creates a pattern. Although some do walk, most people visiting a downtown arrive by car and the first thing they do is park. After parking a car, the driver becomes a pedestrian walking toward a destination. Downtown destinations for pedestrians remain fairly consistent through time and form one element of an access pattern. Parking locations form a second element, and the pedestrian paths between them form a third.

Parking distribution around the core downtown area is the key variable in defining access models, because it not only affects the spatial pattern of mass and void but also determines the route of important pedestrian paths. Each town observed provided similar quantities of parking in relationship to the size of is downtown commercial district, but how the parking locations were arranged varied widely by town. Definitions of access models were based on these arrangements, and the observed opportunities and consequences of each were evaluated.

Calculating the Need for Parking.

A systematic method exists for modeling how much parking is needed in downtowns. Like the methods used to calculate parking in shopping centers and other related uses, it is based on ratios of parking spaces to the floor areas of different types of building uses.[6] How this method is applied to town centers is particularly well documented in *The Parking Handbook for Small Communities*.[7] An analysis of parking demand in an individual town should consider the mix of building uses to create the most accurate model; a typical mix results in a ratio of two public parking spaces required for each one thousand square feet of commercial or institutional floor area. This formula does not include dedicated spaces for employees and residents.

Analysis of the towns in this study determined that their public parking quantities met the standard of two spaces per one thousand square feet of floor area. Quantity also consistently related to the length of commercial and institutional building street frontage in a ratio of twelve spaces for every one hundred feet of frontage.

On-street Parking Proportion

Most towns provide some on-street parking. Parallel parking spaces on both sides of all commercial blocks will supply about half of the public parking needs of a downtown with full ground-floor occupancy. If this base level of on-street parking is provided, then an equivalent amount of additional parking must be provided in off-street lots. When the base level can be exceeded with diagonal parking or other ways to increase on-street parking, then fewer off-street spaces are required. Conversely, if the base level is not met with on-street parking, then more off-street spaces must be provided.

Parking Location and Access Models

Arranging the supply of additional parking sets the patterns for downtown access types. In the thirty-two towns that were field surveyed, five models for arranging the parking supply were identified, along with some hybrids of those models, and a no-model approach. A more extensive group of towns could possibly yield other

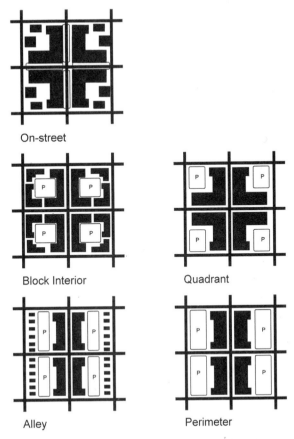

On-street

Block Interior

Quadrant

Alley

Perimeter

Figure 5.5. These conceptual diagrams represent five ways that parking is commonly organized in small downtowns.

models. The models are described below as generalized from several examples. The diagram for each is an idealized layout that illustrates the pattern of parking, buildings, and streets (figure 5.5).

On-street

The on-street model for access is the simplest system for parking and pedestrian access. Highlands, North Carolina; Kearney, Nebraska; and Nevada City, California, are all examples of on-street models. All of these, however, also have a small amount of supplemental off-street parking. Achieving the required quantity of parking on the street requires parallel parking extending into residential areas around the commercial district (as in Nevada City), diagonal parking on every commercial street (as in Kearney), or parking spaces in the center of the street (as in Highlands).

Figure 5.6. Central Avenue, Kearney, Nebraska and Broad Street, Nevada City, California. Diagonal parking spaces on Kearney's wide streets allow a greater number of spaces to be provided on-street. Street parking in Nevada City continues into the neighborhoods around the commercial center, making it possible to minimize off-street parking.

Pedestrian routes use sidewalks on the streets, and no exclusive pedestrian passages are required (figure 5.6).

An alternate form for the on-street model occurs in towns with a courthouse square or park surrounded by commercial streets. The combination of diagonal parking on both sides of the streets and commercial buildings on only one side creates a high ratio of parking quantity to commercial frontage.

Quadrant

Quadrant parking results when each block contributes a portion of the off-street parking supply. The lots are adjacent to the street, usually on the corner farthest from the town center (figure 5.7).

Pedestrian routes use cross streets to connect to the main commercial street(s). Some alleys and pedestrian passages are also used to connect to cross streets.

Perimeter

Perimeter parking encircles the downtown commercial core. Parking lots usually occupy the back edge of the blocks that face the commercial center. In some towns, such as Glenwood Springs, Colorado, parking is interspersed with detached commercial buildings. In others, such as Ames, Iowa, parking forms a nearly unbroken band on the back side of the commercial district. Pedestrian access is usually through an outlet from the parking lot onto a cross street connecting to the town center.

Alley Slot

Alley slot parking occurs in towns that have alleys parallel to the main commercial street. Parking arranged along the alley occupies a swath or slot through the

Figure 5.7. Main Street, Lebanon, Ohio. Parking lots are usually sited on the rear corners of commercial blocks in towns with quadrant parking systems.

Figure 5.8. Franklin, Tennessee. Alley slot parking occupies the space adjoining the alleys in downtown blocks.

middle of the downtown blocks (figure 5.8). Both auto and pedestrian access are typically through the alleys, but pedestrian circulation can be separated into other passageways.

Block Interior

Block interior parking results from inserting parking into the centers of blocks adjacent to main commercial streets. The system requires the consolidation of individual properties in the interior to achieve greater efficiency in parking (figure 5.9). Pedestrian routes out of the block interiors are through gaps in the building pattern along the streets surrounding the block. The placement of the passageways allows people to be distributed into different parts of the downtown.

The Tactical Model: Opportunistic Parking

Many towns have parking arrangements that cannot be fit into a spatial model. In such towns, parking location is based on real estate opportunities. When the demand for parking outstrips the supply, and properties in or near the downtown core

Figure 5.9. New Berne, North Carolina. Consolidation of properties within the interiors of blocks allows the development of efficient public parking areas.

become available for purchase, then parking lots are developed on those sites. The location of the parking supply can become unbalanced because of the concentration of available properties in particular areas. The resulting pedestrian routes vary. Some use alleys to connect lots with side streets, others connect directly to side streets, and some open onto main commercial streets (figure 5.10).

Figure 5.10. North Maple Street, Winchester, Kentucky. Parking locations based on real estate opportunities may be in inconvenient and unappealing locations.

PRESERVATION AND DESIGN CRITERIA FOR ACCESS

The towns visited in this study built their downtown development efforts partially on design quality and preserving the traditional form of their downtowns. When design and preservation values are important, then criteria emphasizing those values should guide access design. These criteria govern convenience, quality of experience, preservation of historic fabric, and connections with neighborhoods.

Convenience and Experience

Shopping center designers work with a premise that shoppers desire to walk 300 feet or less from their car to a store and will accept a maximum of 450 feet.[8] Several other researchers have found that distances within that range also apply to small downtowns.[9]

Measuring walking distance downtown requires an identified destination. For this study, a "commercial center of gravity" was identified in each town. The center of gravity is the center of the area of downtown with the highest building occupancy rate, rental values, and level of maintenance. These locations were identified in the field and confirmed through local interviews. For consistency, the center of gravity is shown as a circle five hundred feet in diameter on the maps. Although located in the field without regard to distances from the edges of the downtowns, the centers were found to be generally symmetrical to the edges of the downtowns when they were placed on maps.

Convenience, as determined by distance between parking and the commercial center of gravity, was evaluated based on 150-foot increments. Although perhaps arbitrary, these divisions were chosen because they agree with the increments commonly used in the related land planning literature.

Quality of pedestrian experience was evaluated based on mapping and photographic documentation of the various routes from parking areas to the commercial centers of gravity (as described in chapter 4). These routes are the essential element of the access experience once the downtown zone has been reached.[10] Positive factors associated with route experience include views to orienting landmarks, early visual contact with business entrances or signs, specifically designed pedestrian ways, and clean and maintained areas adjacent to the route. Negative factors associated with the routes include space shared with service uses or vehicles, lack of commercially activated building facades, and expanses of parking without clear cues for pedestrian circulation.

Preservation: Buildings and Connections to Context

Downtown preservation organizations are concerned not only with buildings but also with the integrity of traditional relationships between buildings and streets. The types of buildings in downtowns vary, but two signature characteristics apply to traditional downtown commercial districts: the higher density of the building pattern and the clear definition of street corridors by buildings. Parking, of course, competes directly with the ground that is, or was, occupied by buildings. The parking areas in each mapped town were overlaid onto Sanborn maps from the 1920s—for many American towns, the last decade when significant numbers of common-wall, no-setback buildings were constructed—to identify buildings that had previously occupied the sites now used for parking.[11]

Any loss of building density can be seen as a negative impact on a downtown from a preservation viewpoint, even when it is replaced with needed parking. These losses, however, vary in significance. Commercial and institutional buildings are greater losses because they could serve contemporary uses of downtown. Industrial, warehouse, livery, and other similar buildings, while still a loss, may be less so because it is more difficult to adapt them to contemporary downtown uses. Buildings with street frontage are generally greater losses because of their role in creating the public environment. An optimal parking scenario maximizes the number of parking spaces while minimizing the destruction of street frontage buildings.

The adjacency of commercial and residential areas is another distinguishing historic quality of small downtowns.[12] Maintaining adjacency of land use is a significant objective of downtown preservation because it is an essential quality not duplicated in other types of commercial development. Adjacency has, of course, also been much discussed by the New Urbanism movement.

Parking areas and access routes play a large role in maintaining the connections between neighborhoods and downtown commercial centers. Parking areas can interrupt connections along streets and destroy adjacency. Well-developed pedestrian routes from parking areas can reinforce connections by serving two groups— those who parked a car and those who walked from a neighborhood.

The strength of each town's connections to its downtown was documented by walking and photographing the street corridors leading into the center. The qualitative strength of connection along the corridors was evaluated by comparing the distances that the corridor was influenced by connecting elements—such as dwellings, commercial buildings, front yards, and street trees—with the distances that the corridor was influenced by parking lots.

INDIVIDUAL MODEL CHARACTERISTICS

Five towns are described here as examples of the access models. These towns were chosen for discussion because they illustrate most clearly the issues raised by each model. The characteristics of each model are summarized in table 5.1.

On-street: Highlands, North Carolina

Highlands is essentially a downtown without parking lots. Parking has been developed to the maximum extent possible on all downtown streets. Main Street (U.S. Highway 64) has a row of diagonal parking in the center and on each side of the street. One travel lane runs in each direction. When parking on Main Street is nearly full and traffic is at its busiest, vehicles are able to flow easily, if slowly, without significant congestion (figure 5.11). The need to stop to allow parked cars to back out, however, would likely raise concerns in many towns.

The most used pedestrian routes are up and down Main Street. Other major routes lead from a large reservoir of on-street parking on Church Street and from the single public parking lot behind the Town Hall.

Table 5.1. Summary of Parking Model Characteristics

	Highlands *On-street*	Lebanon *Quadrant*	Taos *Perimeter*	Franklin *Alley slot*	New Berne *Block interior*
Convenience	**High** 75 percent of parking within 300 feet	**Medium** 50 percent of parking within 300 feet	**Low** Less than 25 percent of parking within 300 feet	**High** 75 percent of parking within 300 feet	**High** 75 percent of parking within 300 feet
Pedestrian Experience	Building fronts Streets	Building rears Passageways Streets	Building fronts Building rears Alleys Streets	Building rears Alleys Passageways	Building rears Passageways
Building Preservation	No displacement of buildings	Parking displaces sheds, stores, and dwellings	Parking displaces dwellings, institutions and garage/livery	Parking displaces sheds, stores, and dwellings	Parking displaces sheds rear additions, and garages
Interruption in Neighborhood Connections	No interruptions	**Medium** Interruptions one half block wide	**Wide** Interruptions one half to full block wide	**Thin** Interruptions one quarter block wide	**Thin** Interruptions less than one quarter block wide
Primary Design Needs	Automobile circulation management Streetscape	Passageways Street edge continuity	Street edge continuity Parking lot appearance	Passageways and alleys Building rear facades and entrances	Passageways Building rear facades and entrances

Figure 5.11. Main Street, Highlands, North Carolina. Main Street in Highlands has diagonal parking in the middle and on both sides of the street.

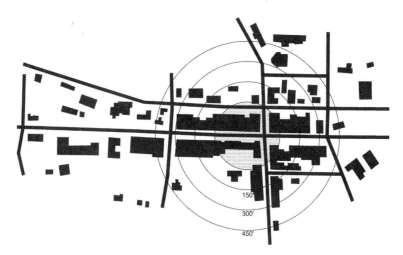

Figure 5.12. Highlands, North Carolina. Highlands' commercial buildings are in a linear pattern on Main Street. The shaded area is the commercial center of gravity. The numbered concentric rings delineate distances in feet from the edge of the center. Linear features are streets, and solid shapes are buildings. Highlands has an extraordinary amount of on-street parking and does not rely on parking lots.

The great majority of the parking spaces in Highlands is within 450 feet of the center (figure 5.12). Those spaces that are farther away are stretched out on the long Main Street and are still in front of retail businesses.

Walking paths in Highlands are predominantly on sidewalks, but several varieties of the sidewalk experience exist. In some places, the sidewalk is elevated above

Figures 5.13, 5.14, and 5.15. Main Street, Highlands, North Carolina. Walking sequences in Highlands are all on sidewalks but include a variety of spatial experiences.

the street; in another, it literally becomes the front porch for a hotel; and in others, it connects with small courts (figures 5.13–5.15). All of the sidewalks incorporate a wide variety of retail facades.

Parking has not displaced buildings in Highlands since it is on the street. During peak parking hours, automobiles become a dominant visual element in the downtown. Parking does not interrupt neighborhood connections in Highlands.

Quadrant: Lebanon, Ohio

Lebanon has four major business blocks that form a set of quadrants surrounding the commercial center of gravity. Each quadrant provides a part of the off-street parking supply. Some of the lots follow the pattern of the idealized model and are carved out of the corner of the quadrant farthest from the center. Others are located across the street from the back side of the quadrant (figure 5.16).

Lebanon has parallel parking on both sides of most downtown streets. The off-street spaces range between 150 feet and 450 feet from the center, with the exception

Figure 5.16. Lebanon, Ohio. In this plan of downtown Lebanon, cross-hatched shapes represent public off-street parking areas.

of one parking area. This lot is completely outside of the 450-foot distance and is almost unused at present.

Most of the parking lot connections in Lebanon are on sidewalks on cross streets. The sidewalks pass by some business facades but mostly by blank side walls of buildings that front on the main commercial street. One parking lot in Lebanon uses a passageway to connect to the center (figure 5.17).

The parking lots in Lebanon are mainly on sites once occupied by dwellings. Nineteen former dwelling sites are used for public parking, along with the sites of eight businesses. Because the quadrant sites face out to the street, all of the removed buildings were ones that framed the street corridor.

The transitional areas between commercial and residential uses in the downtown are affected by the parking locations. Several lateral street corridors that lead into downtown pass by one of the public parking areas, creating an interruption in pattern. The tree plantings around the perimeter of the lots in Lebanon reduce the negative impact that parking has on the sidewalks (figure 5.18).

Figure 5.17. Lebanon, Ohio. Quadrant parking can be connected to commercial centers with pedestrian passageways.

Figure 5.18. Main Street, Lebanon, Ohio. Tree plantings bordering parking areas help maintain continuity of the street corridor.

Perimeter: Taos, New Mexico

The streets in Taos, New Mexico, are narrow and provide for little parking. The major on-street supply is a row of diagonal parking all the way around the outside edge of the streets surrounding the plaza. A mixture of public and private lots that encircle the core downtown and plaza area compensates for the lack of on-street parking (figure 5.19).

Figure 5.19. Taos, New Mexico. In this plan of the town center, the commercial center of gravity is in the plaza.

Pedestrian routes into the center of Taos are through a converging set of alleys and streets that lead from the perimeter into the plaza. The perimeter model has enabled a good distribution of convenient parking in Taos. All of the parking is between 150 and 450 feet of the plaza, with the exception of two outlying lots not shown on the map, which are used for peak tourist periods.

Many of the pedestrian sequences in Taos feel decidedly like back-door approaches. Some pathways are in alleys without walks; the better approaches are on streets. All of the paths offer a high degree of anticipation, which is created by the indirect views into the plaza. The knowledge that the plaza lies ahead compensates for the poor quality of many of the entrance sequences. Towns that use perimeter parking as a model need a highly focused and imageable center to balance the dominance of parking on the edge (figures 5.20–5.22).

Parking in Taos occupies the former sites of various building types, including a church, many attached adobe dwellings, an agricultural products dealer, and other service businesses. Of all the parking sites, the former Guadalupe Church and its plaza have been the greatest loss for Taos.

The pedestrian connections to neighborhoods are affected by passing through parking zones immediately before entering the core of the town center. Most traffic corridors through the center of Taos have been visually affected by perimeter

Figures 5.20, 5.21, and 5.22. Camino de la Placitas, Ranchito Road, and Taos Plaza, Taos, New Mexico. The sequence from the old Guadalupe Plaza parking area into the plaza is a back-street approach, but the experience is enhanced by anticipation of Taos Plaza.

parking areas. Perimeter parking consistently disrupts historic building patterns on perimeter streets, commonly leading to a disconnection from context. In Taos, the small size of the parking areas helps to maintain visual connections.

Alley: Franklin, Tennessee

Franklin, Tennessee, has off-street parking organized along the alleys that bisect the downtown blocks. The parking lots fill a wide slot, parallel with Main Street, down the center of each block (figure 5.23). Like block interior parking, the lots are consolidated from several smaller properties. Pedestrian access out of the lots in Franklin is through the alleys. Little design provision has been made to identify pedestrian space within most of the alleys.

The linear form of the parking allows good distribution of spaces. Because Franklin has a fairly long commercial district, some spaces are farther than 450 feet from the center but are still easily within 300 feet of Main Street. Franklin does not have midblock passages to connect parking areas and the street, so parking in the middle of an alley lot can lead to an extended walk in the alleyway.

Pedestrian-only passageways and shared alleyways in Franklin contrast the best and worst pedestrian experiences that can be had in an alley parking organization (figures 5.24 and 5.25). The pedestrian passages in Franklin connect to the

Figure 5.23. Franklin, Tennessee. In this plan of Franklin, the commercial center of gravity and the town square are separated.

Figures 5.24 and 5.25. Franklin, Tennessee. Pedestrian access to alley parking in Franklin is through both pedestrian passages and the alleys themselves.

square, the downtown's most significant space. The alleyways are narrow, and only one has been improved above the level of a service alley. The alleys connect to cross streets that then lead to Main Street.

Alley parking can avoid building demolition, because most of the parking is placed away from street corridors. In Franklin, the alley parking areas occupy the sites of only seven dwellings and four store buildings. The preservation impacts become greater where the parking areas extend all the way to the cross-street corridor. The worst cases in Franklin are two places where the parking areas widen at the cross street, on the former sites of commercial buildings (figure 5.26).

Figure 5.26. Hopkinsville, Kentucky. The street environment is affected when alley parking extends to the street edge.

Alley parking that respects the cross-street corridors has the potential to improve connections to neighborhood context if it stimulates private investment in buildings along the cross-street connection to the center or public investment in the pedestrian walks on the cross street. In the areas where it widens out at the cross street, alley parking has harms the neighborhood connection. In Franklin, this impact is not mitigated with tree planting.

Interior: New Berne, North Carolina

New Berne, North Carolina, uses block interior parking in combination with its on-street supply. Block interior parking results from consolidating individual properties in the interior of commercial blocks. Combining properties allows greater efficiency in parking layout. In New Berne, the two blocks on either side of the strongest commercial segment of Middle Street have had their interiors carved out for parking (figure 5.27).

Pedestrian routes out of the block interiors are through gaps in the building pattern along the streets surrounding the block. The placement of the passageways allows people to be distributed into different parts of the downtown.

Figure 5.27. New Berne, North Carolina. New Berne has a mix of parking types, but the core of the shopping district is served by a large lot in the interior of a block.

The interior lots in New Berne place the majority of off-street parking within 300 feet of the center of downtown. Distribution could be a problem for outlying blocks without interior lots in some towns; however, in New Berne, on-street parking compensates for the lack of parking lots in some areas. New Berne has one well-designed parking lot outside the 450-foot radius from the center; this lot is virtually empty.

Passageways are required to allow pedestrian traffic onto streets, unless access drives or alleys are used. New Berne has passages designed exclusively for pedestrians in which attention has been given to lighting, planting, and artwork (figures 2.28–2.29). The passageways also allow views from the parking areas directly into the commercial center of the downtown.

The parking areas themselves have replaced storage and work buildings that were behind the downtown retail buildings. Those buildings are a minimal loss to the larger downtown fabric. The automobile and pedestrian passageways require existing openings in the line of commercial buildings or demolition to create an opening.

Figures 5.28 and 5.29. New Berne, North Carolina. Several passages exclusively designated for pedestrians lead out of New Berne's interior lots.

Block interior parking does not interrupt street corridors and so does not directly affect connections to neighborhoods. Because investment may be concentrated into the lots and the connecting passageways, however, the streets that connect neighborhoods with the town center may be neglected.

OBSERVATIONS ON THE RELATIVE STRENGTHS OF THE MODELS

When the towns in this study were first planned and built, pedestrian access was assumed to be relatively evenly distributed on walks on streets leading to the center of the commercial area. Parking of horse-drawn vehicles, and later automobiles, was easily accommodated on the streets. Thriving historic downtowns have been forced to retrofit for increased parking and for pedestrian concentrations on selected pathways as a result of parking location.

Increasing the amount of on-street parking creates the fewest conflicts from a preservation perspective. Towns that increase their on-street parking achieve access retrofit with the least damage to historic properties and with the smallest required investment in pedestrian facilities. Parking cars on streets removes pressure for building demolition. Pedestrian pathways on streets capitalize on downtowns' existing architectural assets.

When towns are required to expand parking off of the street, they begin moving away from the traditional access model. Any expansion of parking off of the street will affect the building fabric and will create new pedestrian experiences. This is a time to plan comprehensively, not incrementally. The need to achieve appropriate parking quantity and location for economic well-being does not override the need to preserve buildings and street corridors and to ensure a high-quality pedestrian environment.

Towns that turn access inside out by bringing parking inside blocks and creating pedestrian connections to streets create less disruption to the historic fabric than those that incrementally expand street parking into the blocks. The block interior model allows buildings on the street to continue to define public space. The pedestrian on the sidewalk experiences only one automobile space, balanced by a wall of commercial buildings. Planning responsibilities and financial costs are greater for interior parking. It requires coordination to assemble parts of many properties to create an interior parking lot. Designing and developing pedestrian passages requires investment and can have consequences for building preservation. Individual property owners become obligated to improve the rear of their buildings and consider new entrances.

Alley slot parking functions similarly but has more impact on the street at the ends of the parking lots that are created. Care should be taken to prevent widening of the parking areas at the ends, so that street-front buildings are retained. A distinct advantage of alley slot parking is that the existing alley is used for the travel lanes, which reduces the amount of land required for the parking area.

Off-street parking adjacent to streets essentially allows streets to push into blocks, creating wider and less even corridors. When streets invade the edges of blocks, both the definition of streets and the architectural continuity of blocks are lost. The quadrant model for parking has this effect by taking the space of dwellings and secondary commercial buildings. In addition, it typically removes corners, which are the most visible portion of a block perimeter as well as the locations most likely to affect walking routes from neighborhoods. The visual impact can be reduced with planted buffers or walls, but the liveliness of the lost buildings cannot be replaced.

The perimeter model is the most difficult to mitigate for pedestrian and visual quality because of its widespread impact. A perimeter pattern for parking can remove the architectural edge on most of the streets at a downtown's edge. The paths from neighborhoods must then pass through the parking zone, and the buildings on the opposite sides of the streets are disconnected from the rest of the building pattern. Perimeter parking can create the least impact, however, on the core of a downtown.

A tactical approach to parking without a particular organizational model has the flexibility to avoid some of the preservation problems associated with the more developed patterns of parking. Because few properties are assembled for parking development in any one location, building destruction may be isolated. Larger and more efficient parking areas hidden from the street can rarely be developed, however, without a greater level of planning. The predictability of location that aids drivers in finding spaces is also more difficult to achieve without an organizational pattern.

Much attention has deservedly been given in recent urban design literature to the desirability of walkable shopping areas and close connections to residential areas. The current reality, however, is that most Americans own and use cars, and that the economics of choice in shopping result in fluid and unpredictable business patterns. This fluidity requires that shopping centers draw customers from outside their own neighborhood to compensate for the loss of shoppers to other places—with great impact on design of parking and circulation.

There is no best model to guide downtown access development. The standardization of suburban shopping centers cannot be achieved with the varieties of downtown forms. The advantages of each access model should be fitted to the formal characteristics of an individual town. Studies by the Urban Land Institute, the Main Street program, and others have made the quantitative calculation of parking needs explicit. Thinking spatially about types of parking and access organizations can encourage the detailing of design issues and preservation costs as well as allow choices to be made in the context of the whole downtown. Towns that examine their opportunities comprehensively have a stronger chance of maintaining valued qualities while achieving access patterns that support their economies.

CHAPTER SIX

Streetscape and Public Space Design Guidelines

This chapter presents design guidelines for implementing plans that resolve the issues discussed in previous chapters. They are intended to crystallize the basic purposes of downtown streetscape and public space design and to offer a framework for meeting functional objectives. The guidelines are loosely written so that they may help simplify solutions rather than further complicate them. However, following the guidelines may require more time spent in planning and design, even as less money might be spent on construction. Specifically, they intend to encourage conservation of historic resources, make public environments that serve residents and visitors to commercial districts, and target investment where needed. The guidelines are written from the perspective of historic preservation theory and policy.

Three terms appear often in the design guidelines:

appropriate: suitable, fitting
compatible: harmonious or agreeable association
contemporary: belonging to the same period of time.[1]

The guidelines build on the above definitions to express a design ethic emphasizing historic authenticity while also encouraging improvement suited to contemporary needs.

Appropriate design in a historic environment is compatible with existing scale, forms, and materials. Appropriate design of elements may be historically authentic, as in the use of the same light standard that was historically used or the repair of building facades to retain the structure of the building as constructed. Appropriate design may also be contemporary, rather than historic. Contemporary design is appropriate if it is compatible in scale, form, and material and is also suitable and fitting for its purpose.

Suitability can be defined by these elements: it accomplishes a particular purpose effectively, it will have longevity of material and style, and it is pleasing in its appearance. The choices involved are clearly subjective, and making design decisions requires careful deliberation.

The physical material of downtowns will always need to be adaptable to helpful changes, such as increased safety or accessibility. Older commercial centers already reflect a continuum of change, and their continued vitality will depend on a preservation focus that integrates contemporary improvements into historic patterns.

The guidelines also reflect two other topics from chapter 1: prospect and refuge, and complexity and legibility. Although these words are not normally used in a town's discussion of design objectives for a streetscape or parking project, the concepts are present in the background and are expressed in other ways. The terms *comfort, unity, variety, rhythm, repetition, focal point*, and *landmarks* are all commonly used to express aspects of the two overriding environmental concepts. These guidelines reflect the need for streets to provide unity and variety in balance as well as a comfortable sense of enclosure and protection balanced by openness and view.

Finally, the design guidelines are driven by basic functional needs: (1) to reconceive streets that are of as much service to pedestrians as they are to cars, (2) for streets and public space to serve a community in multiple ways, and (3) for the entire public infrastructure to facilitate downtown enterprise. Meeting these needs can help achieve the goal of creating walkable communities in which humane patterns of dwelling and commerce can exist.

Before the specific design guidelines are described, three imperatives of design in historic commercial districts should be considered: creating social space, preserving historic architecture while also building compatible infill construction, and maintaining material authenticity in historic commercial districts. Although these imperatives are more about general priorities and a way of thinking about historic downtowns, they also guide more specific decisions and physical results.

SOCIAL SPACE: DESIGN FOR PEOPLE

Our fascination with town centers is only partly about buildings, landscapes, and streets. Their role as the focus of activity and their embodiment of past experiences make them more compelling than their simple presence as physical artifacts. Perhaps we devote so much effort to preserving and revitalizing them because of their ability to gather people together for diverse activities and to become civic places.

If town centers are to be more than a setting for historic buildings and artifacts—that is, if their underlying purpose is to be a setting in which people interact—then design for people must be the primary goal. Design for people in a downtown will make it a place that provides for small social opportunities and larger gatherings, that allows people to move about using various modes of transportation, that has a pleasant sense of congestion resulting from its popularity, and that provides a safe environment.

Different kinds of public spaces have different histories and serve different social needs. Traditional greens, courthouse squares, parks, and commons are typical of older public nonstreet spaces. Because these spaces are historic, preservation philosophy and methodology should primarily guide the design process. Traditional green spaces are appropriate for light use and for occasional larger public gatherings, but if they are largely vegetated, they should be treated with care.

Public plazas of various scales provide space for higher levels of intensity. In smaller communities, the population is usually not large enough to fill a large plaza that does not have other daily uses. Making a plaza part of an important pedestrian connection, creating a linear plaza on the perimeter of a public green space, and surrounding a small public space with retail facades are ways to ensure that a plaza space is available for activities and is also populated day to day. These kinds of public spaces should always be well centered in downtown activity.

Accommodating transportation forms other than personal automobiles stimulates pedestrian activity and reduces the need for car parking in town centers. Public transportation—whether a regular bus service, a van service, or a circulating trolley—should be provided with waiting areas in active, centralized locations. Public plazas often work symbiotically with transit stops to create hubs of activity.

Temporary or transformable spaces enable a town to accommodate specific but occasional functions without having to completely dedicate a place to a single use. Farmer's market facilities can be designed into parking lots or multiuse public spaces in ways that serve both uses (figure 6.1).

Segments of streets can be designed to accommodate pedestrian use and outdoor dining at midday as well as large public gatherings at other times (figure 6.2). If large gatherings—such as street dances, festivals, and other public events—happen only occasionally, then designing a streetscape to accommodate them uses space more effectively than dedicating another area permanently to those activities.

Sidewalks are social spaces . They require great care to maintain their vitality as something more than pedestrian conduits. Sidewalk cafés and outdoor sales areas

Figure 6.1. Showers Common, Bloomington, Indiana. The municipal government building's parking lot in Bloomington, Indiana, is used as space for a farmer's market. The shelters can be parked under when the market is not in session.

Figure 6.2. St. Clair Street, Frankfort, Kentucky. St. Clair Street is often closed to traffic for the midday hours in the warm season and is a popular place to eat lunch.

adjacent to storefronts should be encouraged to create activity and increase social interaction.

Street frontage should be occupied only by those uses that encourage walk-in traffic. Drive-through uses should certainly be located away from major pedestrian streets and paths.

Public space is intended to encourage sociability. Like good hosts in their own homes, designers and town officials should arrange the elements of public space to encourage people to walk, linger, and converse. Places for people to sit should be clustered in ways that allow people to look at one another comfortably, encouraging conversation. Seating should not be thrust out on the sidewalk as isolated benches but should be arranged in ways that provide both prospect and refuge (figure 6.3).

At the same time, public spaces for daily use should be strongly connected to streets and sidewalks. People come downtown to be immersed in the town, not to seek refuge from it.[2] Pedestrian spaces along sidewalks with generous entries or multiple entries, or where the boundary with the sidewalk is indistinct, will feel more connected.

Thermal comfort is needed if people are to linger in a public space. Achieving thermal comfort varies by region and climate. Depending on the climate, a mix of sunny and shaded areas, shelter from excessive wind, or exposure to light cooling breezes may be required. In the mid-Atlantic and Southeast, for example, extending the outdoor season later into the fall and earlier in the spring depends on creating both shelter from wind and exposure to sunlight—essentially, the creation of suntraps. In the same regions, comfort can be extended into the summer by providing shaded areas.

Figure 6.3. Main Street, Louisville, Kentucky. Seating configured at angles that allow people to face one another encourages conversation.

Triangulation is the idea that if two people are given a third thing to entertain them or to provide a focus, then that external focus will act as an ice breaker.[3] Street entertainers often perform this function in cities. In smaller towns, however, street entertainers would find it difficult to make a living. Instead, a downtown farmer's market may provide the needed focus. Other organized activities, such as a free Friday cookout or live music, can also encourage interaction. Fountains, sculptures, and other public art can act as inanimate triangulators.

Food, of course, brings people together and encourages them to linger in most situations. Public space is no exception. Restaurants with carryout service located adjacent to comfortable green spaces, plazas, or other seating areas work symbiotically with those spaces. In many smaller cities, a barbecue smoker or other outdoor food operation provides a focus for a public space at lunchtime. Larger cities with a tradition of sidewalk vendors may offer a variety of food choices in their public spaces. These options should be encouraged because they broaden the opportunities for enjoyment and reinforce the idea that historic commercial districts are good places full of wholesome activity.

Food brings up a last point about social space: some useful social space may be provided privately. Outdoor cafés provide places to sit, populate a district with activity, and provide income for their owners and workers. By rights, not all outdoor social space should require purchasing drinks or meals, but a balanced mix of private and public space expands the ways to enjoy a downtown.

Many of the above ideas about social space were analyzed and described by the great student of public space William H. Whyte in his film and subsequent book *The Social Life of Small Urban Spaces*. Whyte's ideas were specifically derived from the study of spaces in large cities. The basic ideas of comfort, sociability, entertainment, and dining are true everywhere, but a sense of scale and population density needs to apply when working in smaller communities.[4]

ARCHITECTURE: MASS AND SPACE RELATIONSHIPS

In a large-scale view of a commercial district, blocks of buildings are the mass, and streets are the primary open space. Parks and parking lots join streets as open space. Compared with all of the other parts of a town, a downtown is the only place where mass is predominant over space. This is the most important characteristic differentiating a downtown from other areas (figure 6.4).

Building demolition deteriorates the mass-space relationship and makes the experience of downtown streets much less significant as the building line is perforated by parking lots and vacant areas. Views are opened to service areas and to the

Figure 6.4. Lebanon, Ohio. Buildings are black in this plan, and all space not covered with buildings is white. The town center clearly has a concentrated mass of buildings that provide definition to street corridors. The central area is surrounded by much smaller and less densely spaced buildings.

rear facades of other buildings that were not designed to be exposed to public view. Demolition also harms the remaining buildings. Unless they are on a corner, downtown buildings are usually designed with only front and rear walls that were meant to be exposed to weathering and to view. Side walls that are protected by neighboring buildings can deteriorate if the neighboring buildings are removed, leading to progressive structural damage.

The width of downtown buildings often occurs in multiples of original lot widths. For example, in a given downtown, buildings may be twenty-five, fifty, or seventy-five feet wide. Demolition of some of the buildings destroys the rhythmic repetition of dimension, affecting the level of unity provided by the dimensional pattern.

Buildings represent past investment of materials, energy, and human capital. For the most part, historic buildings are composed of brick, wood, iron, and plaster, all of which are closer to an organic state than a synthetic state. The new materials that would replace them would be largely synthetic and represent a higher energy and environmental cost. Historic buildings that are demolished go to landfills, generating an opportunity cost in the loss of existing space and a real cost in their disposal.

Dense building patterns save energy and encourage walking by concentrating multiple activities within walkable distances. No community, historic or not, can be walkable without a level of building and activity density acceptable to its population.

Restoring dense mass-space relationships depends on the construction of new buildings on vacant or underutilized space rather than on the sites of existing buildings. When new construction occurs, it should have street setbacks similar to those of historic buildings and should use similar options for width dimensions. New buildings might appropriately be set back farther than is typical in a district to provide for outdoor cafés or other public space that reinforces the street edge with activity instead of building mass.

Creation of parking lots on former building sites is the primary reason for downtown building demolition. Maximizing the amount of on-street parking and utilizing suitably located vacant space to develop parking—in either surface lots or parking structures—will preempt the perceived need to demolish buildings for parking. Providing quality walking space and encouraging bicycling and public transportation will reduce the demand for parking space.

AUTHENTICITY AND INDIVIDUALITY

An irony of historic downtowns is that the process of highlighting their own historic values can inadvertently lead them to look more and more like other places. Some reasons for this are unavoidable. The architecture of a particular period will look similar. Town forms may be homogenous within regions. But there is also a "revitalization look." This look usually results from excessive self-consciousness on the part of a town.

Idiosyncrasies may be removed to make way for a more sanitized and stereotypical version of downtown streets. Two principles for design can help maintain individuality. The first principle is to stay focused on maintaining historic fabric and authentic design elements (figure 6.5). The other principle is to use high-quality contemporary design for new elements.

The U.S. Secretary of the Interior's Standards for the Treatment of Historic Properties are based on the need to document existing physical conditions and the evolution of space and material through time.[5] The preservation process in general

Figure 6.5. Savannah, Georgia. Small homely elements, such as these bus stop signs can contribute to a place's distinctiveness.

assumes that a community will want to know as much as practically possible about its physical heritage before it engages work that will manipulate that heritage. Field documentation of existing conditions and analysis of historic documents allow historic conditions and their evolution into the present to be understood for a historic commercial district. This can become part of the basis for making informed decisions about the future with an accurate understanding of the relative historic importance of physical fabric.

Downtown preservation organizations are accustomed to standards for preserving building fabric. The doctrine of repair rather than replace, replace in kind if necessary, and select new elements compatible but not imitative is well established.[6]

Street environments and other landscapes are subject to the same ideas. If a town has existing stone curbs that are removed for construction work, they should be salvaged and reused or replaced in kind, if necessary. If a street has brick paving, it should be maintained with accessibility in mind. Extant historic light standards or other functional elements should be maintained, even when they do not all fit with a comprehensive new pattern. Patterns of building mass and open space are the historic spatial framework for downtown districts, and these patterns should also be considered historically significant.

Conserving historic fabric in street environments and public spaces will not only help separate one town from another but will also maintain diversity of construction materials and design elements within a single town. One block may have light standards that differ from another's, or paving materials may be inconsistent. A downtown environment rich in material variety will be more interesting and less likely to become dated to one period.

In the same vein, private property owners should not be coerced or regulated to the point that their buildings and grounds become sanitized and period perfect. Coordinating the design of signs, for example, might involve a sign ordinance that enforces compatibility between advertising signs and the individual architectural patterns of the buildings on which they are placed but that does not specify particular design elements or styles and does not prevent using modern lights. Awnings may be encouraged but with no expectation that they be the same color, size, or pattern.

Providing incentive funds for building rehabilitation and using a design review process to influence design are perhaps the best ways to encourage private improvements that will be individual but compatible with the rest of a downtown. Facade grant programs are a common method for creating incentives. Building or facade-only easements in combination with grants or on their own are another useful incentive. Easements transfer the right to modify a building or its facade in ways that are incompatible with the Secretary of the Interior's Standards out of the owners' hands.[7] These rights are donated to a charitable or governmental preservation organization. The value of the easement is a charitable gift and can be used to reduce income tax. The easement donation may also reduce the taxable value of a property.

Few towns possess the design purity of a single time period. The level of design restriction applied to a historic museum village is inappropriate in the context of a commercial downtown. Design guidelines for incentive funds or facade easements should focus on individual situations and not sap vitality by overregulation.

Contemporary design is constantly changing. If two towns developed streetscape improvement projects ten years apart and both used well-designed contemporary elements, they would look different from each other. If the same two towns used pseudo-Victorian elements, they would resemble each other and each town would have weakened its sense of authenticity. For this reason alone, well-chosen contemporary design elements will maintain a higher level of authenticity. If good design is the standard by which streetscape elements are selected, they will be in harmony with well-designed historic buildings. Choose elements that are compatible in scale, color, and material with surrounding buildings, and seek the visual liveliness that inspired the original builders.

DESIGN GUIDELINES

The design guidelines offer prescriptive directions for designing and organizing downtown elements. Every project will present different circumstances and should result in different design solutions. The guidelines address functional standards, preservation principles, and parameters for design. Design guidelines do not remove the privilege of making design decisions; rather, they provide criteria for considering the appropriateness of specific design decisions involved in a project. The following six subjects are addressed in the guidelines:

- Pedestrian paths
- Parking
- Lighting
- Trees
- Street furniture
- Public art, graphics, and signs

Each of the six guideline sections begins with a statement on general principles, which is followed by specific guidelines that are illustrated where appropriate.

Pedestrian Paths

A downtown—as an activity center—brings many pedestrians near many moving automobiles, so designing for safety is a priority. Sight triangles at intersections should not be impeded by trees, lights, signs, or street furniture, so that pedestrians are clearly seen. Pedestrian and bicycle zones should be clearly delineated. Pedestrian safety should be valued more than vehicular speed and efficiency.

Good sidewalks and pedestrian paths are universally accessible, are visually connected with building interiors, are punctuated by landmarks of various scales, and provide buffers between pedestrians and auto lanes. Investments in improving pedestrian paths should focus on correcting such negative impacts on pedestrian locations and paths as inaccessible interruptions in pathways, poorly maintained or intrusive private properties, and side streets and alleys that serve as major pedestrian routes but have never been designed with pedestrians' experiences in mind.

A goal of every town should be to constantly improve physical accessibility for its population, including elderly and very young residents, disabled people, and those in wheelchairs or pushing strollers. Some improvements, such as curb ramps at every street corner and ramps at steps, are obvious. Others are more subtle and must be discovered by surveying the routes taken by downtown pedestrians and then analyzing the obstacles to a completely accessible route. Such obstacles can be so simple that they may be overlooked, such as a poor paving surface in an alley or inadequate directional signage coming out of a parking lot.

Sidewalks and pedestrian paths are hierarchical: some are more important than others. Walks on major commercial streets, primary neighborhood connections, and walks that connect parking and destinations deserve a higher level of design and should provide for higher pedestrian capacity than walks that are less significant. If one were to survey an entire downtown to evaluate the quality of pedestrian paths (as discussed in chapters 3 and 4), the results might be disappointing. One would be likely to find many unpleasant, dirty, unsafe, inaccessible, or even threatening paths that have important roles in the pedestrian network.

Choices for walk materials should consider the aesthetic context created by buildings and other materials, the level of maintenance required, and the appropriate balance between the unifying effect of material themes and encouraging a diverse materials palate focused on individual properties. All paving surfaces require eventual replacement or, in the case of unit paving materials, resetting. In addition, pavements are frequently cut and patched for utility repairs. Pavement choices should be made with this in mind so that they can be matched or replaced in the future. Historically, decorative features in paving focused as much on individual properties as on repeated unifying features. Allowing differences in pavement type and detail to occur may help avoid a standardized revitalization aesthetic.

Finally, bicycle riders should be considered when designing downtown streets, sidewalks, and parking areas. Utilitarian bicycle travel offers mobility, autonomy, and door-to-door service in urban settings. Bicycle transportation should be encouraged with bicycle lanes where appropriate and bicycle racks in convenient places. The absence of secure bicycle parking is a major deterrent to bicycle transportation.[8] Bicycle racks should not impede pedestrian movement, and their location should not cause conflicts between bicycles and walkers. Design of bicycle parking areas should be coordinated with the design of surrounding areas so that they are part of the design vocabulary of a downtown and not an anomalous feature.

Accessibility

- Audit all walks for pedestrian accessibility.
- Ensure that accessible routes from adjacent neighborhoods or parking areas to downtown destinations and between destinations meet dimensional requirements for accessibility.
- Drop the curbs at all intersections and crosswalks to make them accessible to wheelchairs. Curb ramps should connect directly to the crosswalks; a diagonal ramp should not be built to give access to two perpendicular crosswalks.
- Ensure that all ramp slopes, cross slopes on walks, widths, and other critical dimensions meet the *Accessibility Guidelines for Public Buildings.*[9]
- Stripe or pave crosswalks with materials that allow them to be clearly seen by pedestrians and vehicle drivers. Traditional narrow stripes are not easily seen in all conditions (figures 6.6 and 6.7).
- Maintain clear zones so that a direct linear path unobstructed by street furniture or planting is available (figure 6.8).
- Make sure that public entrances into downtown buildings have accessible connections to walks.

Figure 6.6. Gurley and Montezuma Streets, Prescott, Arizona. Crosswalks paved with contrasting surfaces create a long-lived marking and imply a higher level of respect for pedestrian traffic.

Figure 6.7. Main Street, Ellsworth, Maine. Bold stripes that parallel the direction of a street are more easily seen by drivers than are narrow stripes perpendicular to traffic.

Figure 6.8. Main Street, Ellsworth, Maine. Sidewalk furnishings and plants should be located so that a consistent path clear of obstructions is available.

- Wherever possible, consider additional elements that increase pedestrian safety and convenience. Examples include:
  - walks that are widened at intersections to create shorter crosswalks (figure 6.9)
  - midblock crosswalks on longer blocks where safe crosswalks can be built

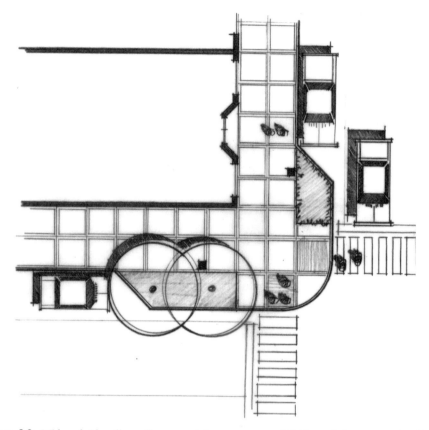

Figure 6.9. Widened sidewalks, or "bump-outs," create greater visibility and shorter crossing distances for pedestrians. Sidewalks widened at corners can also provide sites for plants when narrow sidewalk widths prevent them along the length of blocks.

- low, visually nonobstructive plantings near the ends of crosswalks to bring attention to pedestrian crossings
- improvements in signaling, such as installing pedestrian-activated walk lights and ensuring adequate walk signal time.

Quality of Pedestrian Space

- Audit primary walks for the quality of walking space. The criteria for audits might vary depending on whether a walk segment is a neighborhood connector, connects between parking areas and commercial streets, or is on a commercial spine.
- Connect buildings along primary walks visually to the walks. Windows should allow sight into building interiors, should display merchandise, or should provide other interesting displays.

Figure 6.10. Morton Avenue, Louisville, Kentucky. Parked cars and large pots with plants create a sense of refuge and make a home for café tables outside of a restaurant on a neighborhood street.

- Individual buildings and their signs provide the most visual variety along walks and should be expressive rather than standardized.
- Landmarks at the large scale, such as a clock tower or a prominent corner building, orient pedestrians over a larger area and should be protected or considered in the design of new projects. Smaller landmarks that punctuate a path may result from sidewalk cafés, the color of a building facade, or the design of an unusual sign and should be encouraged.
- Parked cars in parking lanes, streetlamps, street trees, planters, and other furnishings all may help create a sense of refuge from vehicular travel lanes. A sidewalk should not be cluttered, but these elements can be placed strategically to enhance pedestrians' comfort (figure 6.10).
- Building awnings, projecting signs, recessed doorways, and other architectural elements that create undulation in street walls enhance the sense of refuge and create complexity. Retain or incorporate these elements where appropriate.

Bicycle Transportation

- Plan bicycle facilities as part of a connected system linking residential districts and commercial districts. Keep community destinations in mind when planning bike lanes, shared-use paths, and wide curb lanes accommodating bicycle travel.

- Place bicycle racks in locations that are convenient for cyclists and safe for pedestrians. Locate bicycle racks strategically to discourage bicycles being brought onto walks used for shopping, but also conveniently to encourage their use (figure 6.11).

- Bicycle parking may be most appropriately located in larger areas near parking lots, where it may take on a purely utilitarian form. In other situations, it may be distributed throughout a commercial district, where the sculptural character of the racks may become more important (figure 6.12).

- Design all bicycle facilities according to the *Guide for the Development of Bicycle Facilities.*[10]

Materials

- Document the historic or locally traditional paving materials in a particular downtown before making paving choices. Use the historic

Figure 6.11. State Street, Madison, Wisconsin. Where sidewalks are suitably wide, bicycle parking can be conveniently distributed into many decentralized locations. Where sidewalks are narrower, conflicts with pedestrians would result.

Figure 6.12. Fourth Street and Muhammad Ali Boulevard, Louisville, Kentucky. Decentralized bicycle racks, like other street furniture, provide an opportunity to create functional sculptures.

paving material as a model for contemporary paving, if it consists of a material suitable to contemporary construction and accessibility standards.

- If sidewalks or other pathways are rebuilt, retain special existing paving features, including street numbers, steps, building name inlays, and decorative details. Use the same details as a local model for other similar features on downtown walks (figure 6.13).
- Evaluate contemporary decorative paving materials for their compatibility in color and design with existing buildings.
- When selecting paving materials, consider strongly the financial and technical ability to maintain them. Choose paving materials that can be relaid or duplicated in the future when inevitable utility repairs are made.
- Simple pavements, such as well-finished concrete, may be thoroughly appropriate when considered as a background element that allows street furniture, planting, and other features to provide detail (figures 6.14 and 6.15).
- Many advances have been made in porous paving options, so that infiltration occurs through the surface of the paving and runoff is

Figure 6.13. Maysville Street, Mount Sterling, Kentucky. Individualized paving designs can add variety and identify businesses.

Figures 6.14 and 6.15. Main Street, Midway, Kentucky. Plain pavement surfaces provide suitable backdrops for furnishings supplied by businesses.

minimized.[11] Consider porous pavements on walks that are not directly adjacent to building foundations, and in parking areas.

• Consider the financial and environmental costs of different paving materials over their life cycle along with their initial installation cost. Many unit paving materials have a higher installation cost but can be reset or relocated in the future. This lowers their life-cycle cost and requires less energy than producing new paving.

Parking

Parking must be fully considered in downtown design. Parking quantity receives a great amount of attention, but parking organization and management are equally important. Parking should be neither undersupplied nor oversupplied. Problems with undersupply are well-known, but their effect is sometimes exaggerated. Improving multiple modes of transportation, including transit, should be considered as an investment that will offer greater long-term benefits than would creating parking lots to increase access. Oversupply of parking is detrimental because of the negative impact on historic building stock, the wasting of opportunities for infill building construction or public open space development, and the appearance of an underused downtown. Systematically determining actual parking needs balanced with other transportation options and then providing the greatest reasonable proportion of necessary parking on streets will reduce the need for parking lots.

How parking is arranged and designed determines the perception of availability and convenience. Parking areas should be sequenced and signed so that if one lot is full a driver can easily access the next area. Because short walking distances have become normalized by shopping centers, parking should be within 450 feet of the most trafficked and commercially viable areas.

Parking location directly affects the quality of pedestrians' experiences. Parking that is well located and organized will cover two aspects of downtown experience. First, it will be conveniently accessible for a person driving a car and finding a parking space. Second, it will be at one end of a convenient and comfortable walking route when that person is walking on to a destination. The second part is often forgotten, and pedestrians who have just parked a car find themselves walking in poorly maintained alleys, alongside trash containers, and in other undesirable situations.

Negative walking experiences are valid reasons not to return downtown on a subsequent shopping trip. Parking location should be partly determined by the quality of the environment between the potential parking area and the assumed destinations. When parking locations have been determined, the commitment should be made to implement the necessary pedestrian path improvements leading from those locations. These improvements may include pedestrian path paving, landscaping, lighting, and building facade improvements.

Parking Organization

- Do not demolish buildings to create parking.
- Maximize on-street parking. On-street parking is desired enough by shoppers and others that even some traffic constriction is worth having more on-street parking.
- Parking location and design should only minimally affect the continuity of street edges (figure 6.16).
- Organize parking so that it follows a pattern logical for a particular town. Patterns may include expanded diagonal parking on side streets, parking lots in the interiors of all downtown blocks, parking areas lining alleys in the downtown, parking in a predictable location in every block surrounding the center of the downtown, or other arrangements that relate to commercial districts' particular configurations.
- The walking experience after leaving a car in a parking lot should be as convenient as the auto access to the parking. Avoid creating paths through undesirable or threatening areas. Design parking and paths so

Figure 6.16. Main Street, Lexington, Kentucky. Vertical elements at the edges of parking lots maintain the integrity of sidewalk corridors.

Figure 6.17. Versailles, Kentucky. A link between a municipal parking area and a commercial street is made into a courtyard with tables.

that destinations are visible early in the walk. Link paths and downtown park spaces, if possible, to create a lively pedestrian environment (figure 6.17).

- If parking is located behind commercial buildings, coordinate private improvements so that they enhance the aesthetics of the parking area. Building owners should consider creating rear entrances where appropriate.

Parking Design

Parking lots should be designed to fit the needs of automobile drivers and pedestrians, instead of being formed by simply paving over available land. Good parking design requires carefully considering a given site, starting with these basic guidelines.

- Make smaller lots on individual properties more efficient by consolidating them into a single larger lot.
- Two-way travel is preferred in aisles, for greater flexibility.
- Dimension spaces between eight to nine feet wide by 18 to twenty feet long. The travel aisles should be between twenty and twenty-two feet wide.

- Provide adequate numbers of parking spaces for disabled users.[12]
- Include bicycle racks in convenient, visible locations in parking lots, unless bicycle parking can be placed in even more convenient locations near destinations.
- Choose continuous circulation over lot design that has dead-ends and requires drivers to back out when no spaces are available.
- Landscape parking areas appropriately. Emphasize pedestrian areas with planting, paving, or other elements. Provide shade, especially in waiting and drop-off areas.
- Develop islands for shade trees and other landscaping in the interior of all but the smallest (twenty or fewer cars) parking lots. Islands can be many small areas parallel with the parking spaces, or long strips perpendicular to the parking spaces. Use islands at the end of rows of parking spaces to separate parked cars from moving cars (figure 6.18).
- Where parking adjoins a street, develop plantings or structures between the parking area and the street to screen the parking area and to continue the street wall.
- Do not pave the leftover areas created between the parallel edges of a parking layout and the irregular edges of a property; rather, use them for landscaping, pedestrian space, or other creative uses.

Figure 6.18. Lexington, Kentucky. Small urban parking lots can be designed to be tree shaded without significantly sacrificing parking spaces.

- Design accessible pedestrian connections into parking lots. Pedestrians should not be forced to compete with cars at the entrance of a larger parking lot.
- Incorporate multiple pedestrian outlets to allow more efficient foot travel between a parking lot and various destinations.

Lighting

Lighting in a commercial district has several purposes. One is to evenly light travel lanes with the minimum illumination required by state transportation agencies or local ordinance. Pedestrian walks should then be provided with light at a higher level of illumination than the road surface. Lighting is also used to illuminate and accentuate building surfaces, signs, and other features. Lighting from storefront displays can work with sidewalk lights to provide pedestrian illumination. Parking areas, alleys, and public spaces also have light requirements that should be considered in streetscape design.

Light quality is a major component of streetscape quality. Light color, light levels, and evenness of light all affect street character, especially for pedestrians. Warm lighting that allows the colors of materials to be rendered more naturally is preferred over light types that neutralize material colors or that create an excessively cool cast. Excessive light appears harsh and casts deeper shadows, while too little light on sidewalks creates a feeling of insecurity. Lower levels of light emitted from more frequently spaced lights can create even levels of light, cause less glare, and avoid frequent eye adjustment to different light levels.

Lighting should provide for visibility and safety but should also be considerate of the residential aspect of a commercial district. Streets should not be overilluminated to the point that building interiors or private outdoor spaces are negatively affected. Pole height, illumination type, luminaire power, and fixture shape will all affect the amount of light that goes beyond where it is needed. Light pollution also affects people and environments well outside of a commercial district and can be minimized if light is "put where it is needed, during the time period it will be used, and at levels that enhance visibility."[13] Parking lot lighting that can be reduced or turned off during nonbusiness hours and security lighting triggered by movement are two simple ways that energy and darkness can be conserved.

The scale and design of poles and fixtures contribute to the scale of sidewalk space, and pedestrians should be valued when making choices about scale. Many towns historically have had traditional lights scaled for pedestrians, which may have been removed in favor of higher roadway lighting. Such older lights may provide a model for reproduction. Selecting new fixtures requires careful thought to avoid a false sense of historicism.

Style

- If historic light fixtures specific to a downtown can be accurately documented and duplicated, use the historic fixture in a manner similar to its original purposes, locations, and quantities.
- If no documentation is available, or if a historic fixture cannot be duplicated, then use a contemporary pedestrian lighting fixture. Select contemporary fixtures that are compatible in scale and color with the existing architectural features, but do not select them to imitate a historical period (figure 6.19).

Figure 6.19. Maysville, Kentucky. Streetlights can make historic or contextual references while remaining contemporary in character.

- In parking lots and other situations where lighting was not historically present, select contemporary fixtures.
- When historic light fixtures or contemporary pedestrian lighting cannot provide adequate illumination for road surfaces, select unobtrusive contemporary fixtures to provide supplemental street surface lighting.
- Choose or design light poles by considering their use as supports for directional or way-finding signs, banners, traffic signals, or other fixtures to reduce clutter along sidewalks.

Illumination: Height and Placement

- If a historic fixture is used, duplicate the original pole height.
- If a contemporary, pedestrian-scale fixture is used, set the height so that light does not shine into second-floor windows and so that the fixture does not interfere with the view of buildings' sign bands and other architectural features at the top of the first floor.
- If taller fixtures are used to supplement street surface lighting, design their height, placement, and cutoff angle to prevent light trespass into building windows and properties.
- Make sure all light fixtures have an appropriate cutoff angle to reduce glare and night sky light pollution.
- Ensure that light levels are greater at intersections where most pedestrian-vehicular accidents occur.
- Create more even lighting and less glare by using a greater number of fixtures, spaced closer together and with lower-intensity light.
- Use metal halide or other illumination types that produce natural color rendition.
- LED lights provide natural color and are more energy efficient than the traditional outdoor area lighting technologies, but they are currently available for application only to low-height fixtures (generally less than ten feet).

Trees

Trees serve important functional and spatial roles in downtowns. Street trees planted in front of parking lots or other areas without street-edge building facades can help to maintain the traditional mass-space pattern along downtown streets. Tree plantings should be used to maintain the leafy and shaded character of residential zones that have been converted into business uses. Parking lots and downtown parks benefit from shade tree plantings, and trees and shrubs can also be used to screen parking areas. Most towns have places, such as courthouse squares, that were historically landscaped. These areas should be well landscaped and well maintained.

Street trees in consistent rows in the most densely built-up parts of commercial districts commonly conflict with building facades and signage or do not have adequate space for their canopies. Trees often provide more benefits when planted in groups where appropriate and where useful planting sites are available.

Use the period of significance for downtown historic districts as a guide for documenting the history of the downtown landscape. Such historical reference should influence proposed plant material types and locations. But also consider contemporary infrastructure and building conditions.

- Use historic documentation to determine if there were tree plantings associated with particular buildings or areas of the downtown.
- Plant trees only where it is possible to provide the soil volumes necessary to support the intended tree size. A commonly used recommendation in the temperate areas of North America is to provide twenty-five square feet of soil area that has been dug approximately four feet deep (one hundred cubic feet) for a small tree. Trees expected to grow larger need more soil volume. Urban tree authority James Urban recommends a one-hundred-square-foot area dug four feet deep (four hundred cubic feet) for medium and large trees expected to reach maturity.[14] Volumes of this size are available only with continuous tree lawns that may be found in areas on downtown perimeters. This high volume is mentioned to point out the unlikelihood that most downtown street trees will reach a mature size.
- Use trees primarily for environmental improvement—for example, to shade parking lots or to create spatial structure in downtown parks.
- Plant trees in groups or islands of vegetation when possible. Trees thrive in the larger soil volumes provided for a group, and together they shade their own soil, keeping it cooler. Islands in suitable locations can support greater numbers of trees without the conflicts created by rhythmically spaced rows of street trees (figure 6.20).[15]
- Consider carefully the width of walks and the scale of buildings when planning street trees. Dense rows of trees in front of commercial facades can obscure architectural features and signs (figure 6.21).
- Side streets with less articulated building facades may be more appropriate places to plant street trees for visual improvement and for shade, if adequate planting sites can be developed.

Figure 6.20. Public Square, Franklin, Tennessee. Trees have a greater chance to thrive when they are grouped in larger soil volumes.

Figure 6.21. Main Street, Versailles, Kentucky. Closely spaced and densely branched trees can obscure building details and signs.

- Major crosswalks may be appropriate places to widen sidewalks and create planting sites for shrubs; however, shrubs should neither obscure the ability of pedestrians to be seen by motorists nor create potential hiding places.
- Use several different tree species in a single downtown. Monocultural plantings are subject to the same pests and diseases, and one popular species can become repetitive from town to town.
- Choose tree species by considering their mature size and the amount of space available on the site. In most cases, trees should be chosen whose mature size will fit within the volume constraints of a site. Tree species that are chosen strictly on this standard, however, may sometimes be the wrong choice. There are situations where the form of a larger tree species is best suited for a particular site and purpose; in those cases, planned removal and replacement must take place at the appropriate time.
- Except in open park spaces, many urban trees will never reach ultimate mature size before they die or are removed. Street trees, in particular, require periodic replacement.
- Consider carefully the branching structure and foliage density of tree species. Many commonly used urban trees are small in size but are so dense that, instead of framing space, they fill space and obscure views. Denser trees are also more likely to support bird nesting (figure 6.22).

Figure 6.22. Quincy Market, Boston, Massachusetts. Open-crowned trees that can be pruned for higher branching create a canopy, shade pedestrians, and allow building facades to be seen.

- Ensure that planted trees meet the guidelines of the *American Standard for Nursery Stock.*[16]
- Prune trees according to the standards of the Tree Care Industry Association.[17]

Street Furniture

Street furniture includes such elements as benches, trash containers, tree guards, bike racks, aboveground planters, and various historic elements. Street furniture serves direct functions, including providing a place to dispose of trash. Its placement also helps strengthen the refuge quality of sidewalk space and provides sculptural interest. Select and place street furniture so that it serves its purpose as effectively as possible. Effective placement of elements should be based on an understanding of existing and desired patterns of use. Good-quality furnishings are expensive and should be carefully targeted to those places where they are most needed.

Choosing or designing street furniture can employ various strategies. One is to select a coordinated system that influences the tone of streets and walks with consistency. This approach might be considered where there are significant breaks in the consistency of building patterns and where streetscape treatment is needed to reestablish a sense of spatial order. Another approach is to design a variety of different streetscape elements that become art pieces in their own right. This approach might be particularly appropriate where order is already apparent in building patterns and there is more of a need to create variety and anticipation in a streetscape treatment.

Historic street furniture offers tangible connections to the past and sculptural potential, so it has great value in streetscape design.

Style

- Evaluate extant historic street furniture for its ability to remain serviceable. Although they may not become part of a pattern of new street furnishings, individual elements give identity to downtowns. Strive to repair existing elements if they have historic value.
- If duplicates or reproductions of extant or accurately documented historic street furnishings can be produced, consider these rather than stock furnishings.
- Avoid period furnishings, such as "mock Victorian" styles.
- When reproductions of historic furnishings are not possible to document or produce, use compatible contemporary elements. Contemporary furnishings should be compatible in scale and color with existing architectural and landscape features.

Figure 6.23. Main Street, Louisville, Kentucky. Furniture does not have to be chosen from a catalog. These stone seats were designed for a specific location and contribute to its distinctiveness.

- Designing furniture that is unique to a town offers a way to create more timeless elements that are less likely to be dated to a period and are more likely to provoke visual awareness (figure 6.23).

Placement

- Street furnishings should not obstruct pathways.[18]
- Emphasize functionalism in placement. Avoid placing furnishings only to create patterns of design elements. Use benches and other seating to create functional seating groups in downtown parks or other pleasant places to sit. Placing benches in inhospitable locations, where they are unlikely to be used, is wasted effort.
- Consider movable chairs and other furnishings that allow people to create configurations to match their needs of the moment. These have been used successfully in many public spaces as well as sidewalk cafés.
- Consolidate the location of newspaper boxes, mailboxes, and similar functional elements on sidewalks wherever possible.
- Do not allow express delivery service dropoffs and similar elements to cause the removal of parking spaces or narrowing of the sidewalk.

Their design and placement should involve both aesthetic and safety considerations.

Public Art, Graphics, and Signs

Public art, graphics, and signs represent a visual continuum from provocative to the entirely mundane. Highway signs are, and probably should remain, mundane. Private signs and public art, on the other hand, should be used to create a lively visual environment while they serve their purposes.

Public art is often thought of as a way to cover up ugly buildings with murals. The higher calling for artwork in public spaces and streets is to activate or bring focus to those spaces in interesting ways. Art can provoke discussion, be humorous, or communicate the connections between places and the people who live in them.

Private signs are placed because they advertise businesses, but they have other potential as well. Signs are a form of graphic design, and sometimes of sculptural design. If they are treated as an art form that provides information, they can contribute strongly to the complexity and variety in street environments.

Private signs are mounted most frequently on buildings in historic commercial districts, so they also need to work within the geometry of building facades.

Public signs that give directions to automobile drivers should intrude minimally in the downtown. Wherever possible, consolidate groups of signs or eliminate redundant signs. Make other public signs that direct pedestrians or help with way finding more interesting and eye-catching.

Public Art

- Art used to cover up negative aspects of a street or building wall frequently has the opposite effect of calling attention to it. In these situations, find a more fundamental solution to correct the problem, or leave them unadorned so that they are passed with less notice.
- Use public art to organize or enliven public spaces. Art placed where people congregate or pause will have greater impact and create more enjoyment.
- Preserve public art that is historic to a town on its original site and keep its sense of context intact.
- Consider presenting artifacts of a town's past—such as old horse troughs, bells, or industrial relics—as art pieces (figure 6.24).
- Remember that art does not have to be serious or clearly understood. Often, the art pieces that are most enjoyed are humorous or provoke discussion (figure 6.25).

Figure 6.24. River Promenade, Indianapolis, Indiana. An unused rosette from a stone carving factory is incorporated into a wall as an art piece.

Figure 6.25. Showers Common, Bloomington, Indiana. Art's intent is not always clear or serious, as exemplified by this giant coil pot in Bloomington.

Figure 6.26. Maysville, Kentucky. Local connections can infuse art with greater meaning. Hundreds of tiles made by the children of Maysville line a walkway through the town's floodwall.

- Art that is historical or memorial in purpose has an important place in historic commercial districts and has greater visual impact than informational markers.
- Art with a strong local connection may be well received and has the potential to be part of the future history of a community (figure 6.26).
- Public art, whether two or three-dimensional, should be subject to review and consensus in terms of its spatial organization, should represent high standards of design and execution, and should consider issues of maintenance and longevity. It is rare, however, that high-quality art pieces themselves result from consensus. Once the stage is set, the artist should be allowed to work.

Private Sector Signs

- Design control of private signs should not be looked at strictly from the viewpoint of what is allowed. Encouraging a variety of individually designed signs serves many commercial districts well.
- Most downtowns' commercial buildings do not represent a single time period or style. Private signs, like the buildings, should represent a

Figure 6.27. Main Street, Camden, Maine. A pleasant lack of coordination allows business signs in Camden to contribute variety to its main commercial street.

range of styles, periods, or individual preferences. Ensure that sign ordinances are adaptable enough to allow creative use of design and materials and do not force a uniform appearance (figure 6.27).

- The most important basis for restricting sign design is the sign's relationship to the building on which it is placed. Consider carefully whether signs on commercial properties fit within architectural spaces and features. Sign ordinances should not rely on strict dimensional restrictions that are unrelated to how signs fit within the appropriate area on a specific building.

- Most historic commercial buildings have a "sign logic" that should be considered in design. The following elements are appropriate on different buildings:

  - Sign bands should be utilized where available (figure 6.28).
  - Larger-facade panels above the first-floor windows may be the most appropriate place for signs on single-story buildings. In this case, larger signs that are well proportioned to the facade panel may enhance the presence of a small building (figure 6.29).
  - Where transom windows have been removed, the transom location may be appropriate for placing a sign and offers a generous area.

Figure 6.28. Main Street, Midway, Kentucky. Many traditional commercial buildings have sign bands designed specifically for advertising.

Figure 6.29. Main Street, Midway, Kentucky. A plain building panel is a backdrop for a well-proportioned sign.

Figure 6.30. Limeston Street, Lexington, Kentucky. Traditional fabric awnings are not restricted to traditional artwork.

- Functional fabric awnings are traditional locations for business identification. Narrow-width plastic awning signs are incompatible with historic buildings (figure 6.30).
- Window signs may be more appropriate than a sign that intrudes on architectural features. Simple window signs are often used in conjunction with other signs. Window signs should preserve transparency. Well-designed window displays should be integrated with window graphics (figure 6.31).

- Unarticulated side walls of buildings have historically been used for painted advertising signs. Preserve such signs where extant. Consider opportunities to develop new signs in a similar manner through conditional use or variance provisions in sign ordinances. With due caution, investigate sign ordinances for allowances for historic signing techniques in downtown areas.
- Make sure sign materials are of a quality and material type that is appropriate to the building fabric on which they will be placed.
- Do not encourage that private signs be voluntarily coordinated into a uniform design system.

Figure 6.31. Main Street, Midway, Kentucky. A commercial window can coordinate interior display and applied artwork or typography to create a complete composition.

Public Sector Signs

- Consider consolidating or simplifying street signs or regulatory signs as part of a streetscape plan; placement normally requires approval from state transportation agencies (figure 6.32).
- Ensure that all regulatory traffic signs and street name signs consider the *Manual on Uniform Traffic Control Devices.*[19]
- Coordinated traffic light and sign-mounting arms can help reduce visual clutter and the need to look in several places for directional signs (figure 6.33).

Figure 6.32. Lincoln Square, Hodgenville, Kentucky. Public signs that accrete over time can create clutter and be impossible to read quickly.

Figure 6.33. Main Street, Danville, Kentucky. Directional signs organized onto a traffic light arm are removed from the pedestrian environment but remain visible to vehicle drivers.

- Way-finding systems are ways to actively help people make sense of their environment and feel more confident when negotiating a commercial district. Implementing a way-finding system is an important way to welcome people to a commercial district and help make them comfortable.
- Way-finding systems should consider multiple scales of information and the best locations for each. Comprehensive directories, directions to significant individual locations, identification of districts or areas, identification of public parking, and directories of individual blocks are some examples of different scales of information. Locational strategies should carefully target information to places where it is most needed (figure 6.34).

Figure 6.34. Sixth Street, Louisville, Kentucky. A small kiosk is part of a complete pedestrian way-finding system.

- Way-finding fixtures should be designed for longevity and continuity of imagery but should also be adaptable to change. Business names and locations, for example, should be simple to update.
- Do not use way-finding systems as a substitute for good environmental design; they should be only one component part of it.
- Consider carefully the need for banners or other similar public decoration before they are implemented. Banners are often needed only as a substitute for lively building facades and advertising signs. They require a continuing funding commitment, and the same amount of money spent on building facades may create more visual improvement.
- Make the scale of banners, if used, proportional to other streetscape elements. Consider the scale of the panel, the height of mounting, and the scale of the objects on which they are mounted.

This book began with a foundation of design philosophy and has ended by describing the detailed design elements that implement public space plans. This is the proper relationship between the topics, because establishing clear intentions and the strategies for realizing them will always be more important than the details. Sustaining and enhancing their role as the social hearts of their communities is really not about streetscape construction projects; it is about a continuing commitment to the quality of civic life.

This will allow town centers to go on doing what they always have done best: providing space for people to be together in community, allowing commerce to occur as unfettered as possible, representing a cooperative venture that creates and sustains opportunities for individuals, including and celebrating idiosyncrasy, commemorating place and heritage, and providing a focus for the neighborhoods that surround them.

Town centers may play an increasingly important role in the future of North America as rediscovered opportunity centers for metropolitan populations that encompass smaller communities, and where the edges of the metropolitan region are increasingly distant from the main commercial center. In other regions farther away from cities, small-town centers are the only places that offer the balanced mix of public and private activity that is a hallmark of community.

Citizens, entrepreneurs, politicians, and administrators need to understand their town, must share a vision for its future, must love it, and must critically evaluate its weaknesses if a town's historic commercial center is to reach and stay at its potential.

Notes

1. A Philosophical Basis for Downtown Design

1. John Jakle has written or coauthored several books dealing with elements of small-town built environments, including houses, restaurants, gas stations, and motels. Richard Francaviglia's book *Main Street Revisited: Time, Space, and Image Building in Small-town America* (Iowa City: University of Iowa Press, 1996) is a history of the image of the small town in U.S. culture.

2. The journal *Small Town* published many articles over the years dealing with design issues in small towns but was discontinued in 2001. Harry Garnham's book *Maintaining the Spirit of Place* (Mesa, AZ: PDA Publishers, 1985) is one of the few books that discuss an urban design process for smaller communities.

3. Stephen Kaplan and Rachel Kaplan, *Cognition and Environment: Functioning in an Uncertain World* (New York: Praeger, 1982); Jay Appleton, *The Experience of Landscape* (London: Wiley, 1975).

4. Kaplan and Kaplan, *Cognition and Environment*, 5.

5. Kaplan and Kaplan, *Cognition and Environment*, 64.

6. Kaplan and Kaplan, *Cognition and Environment*, 51.

7. Kaplan and Kaplan, *Cognition and Environment*, 77.

8. Kaplan and Kaplan, *Cognition and Environment*, 78.

9. Kaplan and Kaplan, *Cognition and Environment*, 80.

10. Kaplan and Kaplan, *Cognition and Environment*, 72.

11. Kaplan and Kaplan, *Cognition and Environment*, 82.

12. Kaplan and Kaplan, *Cognition and Environment*, 86.

13. Kaplan and Kaplan, *Cognition and Environment*, 84.

14. Thomas Sharp, *Town and Townscape* (London: Murray, 1968), 12–13 (emphasis in original).

15. Bernard Rudofsky, *Streets for People: A Primer for Americans* (New York: Van Nostrand Reinhold, 1969), 241. The illustration in figure 1.8 is a modified version of a map in Rudofsky (p. 241).

16. Appleton, *The Experience of Landscape*, 222–23.

17. Appleton, *The Experience of Landscape*, 223.

18. Stephen R. J. Sheppard, "Beyond Visual Resource Management: Emerging Theories of an Ecological Aesthetic and Visible Stewardship," in *Forests and Landscapes: Linking Ecology, Sustainability, and Aesthetics*, ed. S. R. J. Sheppard and H. W. Harshaw (Wallingford, Oxfordshire, UK: CABI Publishing, 2000), 153.

19. Appleton, *The Experience of Landscape*, 210.

20. William H. Whyte, *The Social Life of Small Urban Spaces* (New York: Project for Public Spaces, 1980), and Clare Cooper Marcus and Carolyn Francis, *People Places: Design Guidelines for Urban Open Space* (New York: Van Nostrand Reinhold, 1990), make many observations and recommendations on configuring downtown open space.

21. National Park Service, *National Register Bulletin 15: How to Apply the National Register Criteria for Evaluation* (Washington, DC: National Park Service, n.d.), 46.

22. National Park Service, *National Register Bulletin 15*, 46.

23. Quoted in David Lowenthal, "Age and Artifact: Dilemmas of Appreciation," in *The Interpretation of Ordinary Landscapes*, ed. D. W. Meinig (New York: Oxford University Press, 1979), 124.

24. Lowenthal, "Age and Artifact," 109.

25. Herb Stovel, "Scrape and Anti-scrape: False Idols on Main Street," *APT Bulletin* 17, no. 3/4 (1985): 53.

26. David Lowenthal, "The Heritage Crusade and Its Contradictions," in *Giving Preservation a History: Histories of Historic Preservation in the United States*, ed. Max Page and Randall Mason (New York: Routledge, 2004), 19–43.

27. Francaviglia, *Main Street Revisited*, 171–73.

28. Golden Ink, "Helen Reborn," http://ngeorgia.com/travel/helen/helen15.html (accessed September 6, 2006).

29. Lowenthal, "Age and Artifact," 125.

30. David Hamer, *History in Urban Places: The Historic Districts of the United States* (Columbus: Ohio State University Press, 1998), 91.

31. Camillo Sitte, *The Art of Building Cities*, trans. Charles T. Stewart (1889; reprint, New York: Reinhold, 1945), 121; Frederic C. Howe, "The City as a Socializing Agency: The Physical Basis of the City: The City Plan," American Journal of Sociology 17, no. 5 (1912): 590–601, quotes at 591 and 601; Ralph Walker, introduction to Sitte, *The Art of Building Cities*, vii and viii.

32. Francaviglia, *Main Street Revisited*, 154.

33. Kevin Lynch, *The Image of the City* (Cambridge: MIT Press, 1960), 83.

34. Francaviglia, *Main Street Revisited*, 157.

35. J. B. Jackson, "To Pity the Plumage and Forget the Dying Bird," in *Landscapes: Selected Writings of J. B. Jackson*, ed. Ervin H. Zube (Amherst: University of Massachusetts Press, 1970), 136–37.

36. Hamer, *History in Urban Places*, 92.

37. Lowenthal, "Age and Artifact," 116.

38. Hamer, *History in Urban Places*, 93–94.

39. Hamer, *History in Urban Places*, 87.

40. David W. Meinig, "Symbolic Landscapes: Models of American Community," in *The Interpretation of Ordinary Landscapes*, ed. D. W. Meinig (New York: Oxford University Press, 1979), 165–67.

41. Meinig, "Symbolic Landscapes," 165–66.

42. Hamer, *History in Urban Places*, 155.

43. Hamer, *History in Urban Places*, 37.

44. Hamer, *History in Urban Places*, 153.

45. Hamer, *History in Urban Places*, 166.

46. Jane Jacobs, *The Death and Life of Great American Cities* (New York: Random House, 1961), 269.

47. Donna J. Seifert, "Defining Boundaries for National Register Properties" (National Park Service, 1997), http://www.cr.nps.gov/nr/publications/bulletins/boundaries (accessed September 12, 2006).

48. Jacobs, *The Death and Life of Great American Cities*, 257–69.

49. Congress for the New Urbanism, "Charter of the New Urbanism," http://www.cnu .org/cnu_reports/Charter.pdf (accessed September 6, 2006).

2. Space and Land Use Configuration in Historic Commercial Districts

1. Dwight W. Hoover, *A Pictorial History of Indiana* (Bloomington: Indiana University Press, 1980), 57.

2. John W. Reps, *The Making of Urban America: A History of City Planning in the United States* (Princeton, NJ: Princeton University Press, 1965), 392.

3. Thomas A. Clark, *A History of Kentucky* (Ashland, KY: J. Stuart Foundation, 1992), 90.

4. J. R. R. Tolkien, *The Fellowship of the Ring* (New York: Houghton Mifflin, 1954), 7.

5. Clara Egli LeGear, *United States Atlases: A List of National, State, County, City, and Regional Atlases in the Library of Congress* (Washington, DC: Library of Congress, 1950), iii.

6. Bates Harrington, *How 'Tis Done: A Thorough Ventilation of the Numerous Schemes Conducted by Wandering Canvassers, Together with the Various Advertising Dodges for the Swindling of the Public* (Chicago: Fidelity Publishing, 1879).

7. LeGear, *United States Atlases*. Two bibliographies of county histories are also useful, partly because they include many county atlases in their listings. One is Clarence Stewart Peterson, *Consolidated Bibliography of County Histories in Fifty States in 1961, Consolidated 1935–61* (1963). The other is Thomas Lindsley Bradford and Stanislaus Vincent Henkels, *The Bibliographers Manual of American History: Containing an Account of All State, Territory, Town and*

County Histories Relating to the United States of North America, with Verbatim Copies of Their Titles, and Useful Bibliographical Notes, Together with the Prices at Which They Have Been Sold for the Last Forty Years (1907–10).

8. University of Iowa Libraries, Iowa Digital Library, http://digital.lib.uiowa.edu/cdm4/index_maps.php?CISOROOT=/maps (accessed February 6, 2008).

9. R. Philip Hoehn, William S. Peterson-Hunt, and Evelyn L. Woodruff, *Union List of Sanborn Fire Insurance Maps Held by Institutions in the United States and Canada,* 2 vols. (Santa Cruz, CA: Western Association of Map Libraries, 1976–77), 1:vi.

10. Hoehn et al., *Union List of Sanborn Fire Insurance Maps,* vi.

11. Walter W. Ristow, *Fire Insurance Maps in the Library of Congress: Plans of North American Cities and Towns Produced by the Sanborn Map Company: A Checklist* (Washington, DC: Library of Congress, 1981), 5.

12. Diane L. Oswald, *Fire Insurance Maps: Their History and Applications* (College Station, TX: Lacewing, 1997), 36.

13. Sanborn Map Company, *Surveyors Manual for the Exclusive Use and Guidance of Employees of the Sanborn Map Company* (New York: Sanborn Map Company, 1923), 4.

14. Oswald, *Fire Insurance Maps: Their History and Applications,* 38, quotation from the *Sanborn Survey* newsletter.

15. Digital Sanborn Maps, 1867–1970, http://sanborn.umi.com (accessed February 6, 2008).

16. Hoehn et al., *Union List of Sanborn Fire Insurance Maps.*

17. Ristow, *Fire Insurance Maps in the Library of Congress.*

18. Hal Morgan and Andreas Brown, *Prairie Fires and Paper Moons: The American Photographic Postcard, 1900–1920* (Boston: Godine, 1981).

19. Nigel Gosling, *Nadar* (New York: Knopf, 1976), 13.

20. Gosling, *Nadar,* 16–17.

21. National Archives and Records Administration, "General Information Leaflet 26," http://www.archives.gov/publications/general-info-leaflets/26.html#aerial1 (accessed November 28, 2006).

22. Julie Campoli, Elizabeth Humstone, and Alex MacLean, *Above and Beyond: Visualizing Change in Small Towns and Rural Areas* (Chicago: Planners Press, 2002).

23. The seventeen towns included Carrollton, *Danville,* Harrodsburg, *Henderson, Hodgenville, Jackson, Lexington (Chevy Chase neighborhood), Pikeville, Russellville, Versailles,* and *Winchester,* Kentucky; *Brookville,* Madison, and Noblesville, Indiana; *Lebanon,* Ohio; and *Franklin* and Murfreesboro, Tennessee. The twelve towns in italics were studied for all time periods; the remaining five were observed only for contemporary development patterns.

24. Richard Lingeman, *Small Town America: A Narrative History, 1620–The Present* (Boston: Houghton Mifflin, 1980), 258.

25. Department of the Interior, Census Office, *Statistics of the Population of the United States at the Tenth Census (June 1, 1880)* (Washington, DC: Government Printing Office, 1882); U.S. Department of Commerce, Bureau of the Census, *Fifteenth Census of the United States, 1920* (Washington, DC: Government Printing Office, 1931).

26. Lingeman, *Small Town America*, 395.

27. Walter Kulash, "The Third Motor Age," *Places* 10, no. 2 (1996): 44.

28. Lingeman, *Small Town America*, 295.

29. Carol Rifkind, *Main Street: The Face of Urban America* (New York: Harper and Row, 1977).

30. John D. Cushing, "Town Commons of New England," *Old-time New England*, 51, no. 2 (Winter 1961): 92.

31. Wal-Mart has a floor area of approximately 225,000 square feet, and Kroger is approximately 75,000 square feet.

32. To create a base area for analysis, the *historic business area* was mapped for each town. This is the area where 75 percent or more of the ground-level building floor area was in business use in the period around 1925. Within the historic business area, blocks or partial blocks with 75 percent or more of the historic building mass still standing were identified as the *architectural core*. Also within the boundaries of the historic business area, blocks or partial blocks with less than 75 percent of the historic building mass still standing were identified as the *parking and service zone*. This is the zone of apparent decline in commercial buildings and commercial activity. Outside of the boundaries of the historic business area, blocks where 75 percent or more of the ground-level building floor area was in business use were identified as the *business expansion zone*. This is the zone of commercial replacement of other land uses, which were mainly residential.

33. Richard Russo, *The Risk Pool* (New York: Random House, 1988), 288.

34. Dolores Hayden, "Urban Landscape History: The Sense of Place and the Politics of Space," in *Understanding Ordinary Landscapes*, ed. Paul Groth and Todd W. Bressi (New Haven, CT: Yale University Press, 1997), 112.

35. Gordon Cullen, *The Concise Townscape* (London: Architectural Press, 1961), 17.

36. Christian Norberg-Schulz, *Genius Loci: Towards a Phenomenology of Architecture* (New York: Rizzoli, 1980), 11.

37. Harry Launce Garnham, *Maintaining the Spirit of Place: A Process for the Preservation of Town Character* (Mesa, AZ: PDA Publishers, 1985), 82.

38. Randolph T. Hester Jr., "The Sacred Structure in Small Towns: A Return to Manteo, North Carolina," *Small Town* 20, no. 4 (January–February 1990): 4–21.

3. Connections: Neighborhood and Downtown

1. Charles Mulford Robinson, *City Planning, with Special Reference to the Planning of Streets and Lots* (New York: G. P. Putnam's Sons, 1916), 81.

2. John Nolen, *Replanning Small Cities: Six Typical Studies* (New York: Huebsch, 1912), 43.

3. Richard Lingeman, *Small Town America: From 1620 to the Present* (New York: Putnam, 1980), 280.

4. Lingeman, *Small Town America*, 292.

5. U.S. Department of Health and Human Services, *Physical Activity and Health: A Report*

of the Surgeon General, U.S. Department of Health and Human Services (Atlanta: Centers for Disease Control and Prevention, National Center for Chronic Disease Prevention and Health Promotion, 1996).

6. City of Portland, *Portland Pedestrian Master Plan* (Portland, OR: City of Portland, 1998).

7. Anne Vernez Moudon, Paul Mitchell Hess, Julie M. Matlick, and Nicholas Pergakes, "Pedestrian Location Identification Tools: Identifying Suburban Areas with Potentially High Latent Demand for Pedestrian Travel," *Transportation Research Record 2002*, vol. 1818, 94–101.

8. Moudon et al., "Pedestrian Location Identification Tools."

9. 2000 US Census Bureau data analyzed with ESRI ArcGIS software.

10. Wendy C. King, Jennifer S. Brach, Steven Belle, et al., "The Relationship between Convenience of Destinations and Walking Levels in Older Women," *American Journal of Health Promotion* 18, no. 1 (September/October 2003), 74–82.

11. Linda S. Dixon, "Bicycle and Pedestrian Level of Service Performance Measures and Standards for Congestion Management Systems," *Transportation Research Record 1996* 1538:1–9.

12. James Emery, Carolyn Crump, and Phillip Bors, "Reliability and Validity of Two Instruments Designed to Assess the Walking and Bicycling Suitability of Sidewalks and Roads," *American Journal of Health Promotion* 18, no. 1 (September/October 2003), 38–46.

13. 2000 US Census Bureau data analyzed with ESRI ArcGIS software and compared with 1950 Sanborn maps of Lexington.

14. John Jakle, Robert Bastian, and Douglas Meyer, *Common Houses in America's Small Towns: The Atlantic Seaboard to the Mississippi Valley* (Athens: University of Georgia Press, 1989).

15. Louisville Metro Government, *Cornerstone 2020 Land Development Code*, http://www .louisvilleky.gov/planningdesign/cornerstone+2020.htm (accessed February 7, 2008).

4. Walking Downtown: The Visitor's Experience

1. Edmund N. Bacon, *Design of Cities* (New York: Viking Penguin, 1974), 35.

2. Bacon, *Design of Cities*, 34.

3. Kenneth T. Jackson, *Crabgrass Frontier: The Suburbanization of the United States* (New York: Oxford University Press, 1985), 52.

4. Geoffrey Baker and Bruno Funaro, *Shopping Centers—Design and Operation* (New York: Reinhold, 1951), 44.

5. Baker and Funaro, *Shopping Centers*, 32.

6. Urban Land Institute, *Shopping Center Development Handbook*, 2nd ed. (Washington, DC: Urban Land Institute, 1985).

7. Kevin Lynch, *Site Planning*, 2nd ed. (Cambridge, MA: MIT Press, 1971), 331.

8. Booth Tarkington, *The Gentleman from Indiana* (New York: Grosset and Dunlap, 1899), 6.

9. Gordon Cullen, *The Concise Townscape* (New York: Van Nostrand Reinhold, 1961), 54.

10. Kevin Lynch, *The Image of the City* (Cambridge, MA: MIT Press, 1960), 97.

11. Richard K. Untermann, *Accommodating the Pedestrian* (New York: Van Nostrand Reinhold, 1984), 27.

12. Cullen, *The Concise Townscape*, 17.

5. The Arrangement of Parking: A Design Perspective

1. Victor Gruen, *The Heart of Our Cities* (New York: Simon and Schuster, 1964).

2. Kent Robertson, "The Status of the Pedestrian Mall in American Downtowns," *Urban Affairs Quarterly* 26, no. 2 (1990): 250–73; Kent Robertson, "Downtown Redevelopment Strategies in the United States: An End-of-the-century Assessment," *Journal of the American Planning Association* 61, no. 4 (1995): 429–37.

3. Gordon Cullen, *The Concise Townscape* (New York: Van Nostrand Reinhold, 1961).

4. Harry L. Garnham, *Maintaining the Spirit of Place* (Mesa, AZ: PDA Publishers, 1985); James F. Barker, Michael W. Fazio, and Hank Hildebrandt, *The Small Town as an Art Object* (Oxford, MS: Center for Small Town Research and Design, 1975).

5. Bert Stitt, "The Lies of Downtown: A Look at the Myths That Keep Downtowns from Engaging in Effective Revitalization," *Small Town* 27, no. 4 (1996): 18–25.

6. Urban Land Institute, *Parking Requirements for Shopping Centers: Summary Recommendations and Research Study Report* (Washington, DC: Urban Land Institute, 1982); Parking Consultants Council, National Parking Association, *The Dimensions of Parking*, 2nd ed. (Washington, DC: Urban Land Institute and National Parking Association, 1983).

7. John D. Edwards, *The Parking Handbook for Small Communities* (Washington, DC: National Main Street Center and Institute of Transportation Engineers, 1994).

8. Kevin Lynch, *Site Planning*, 2nd ed. (Cambridge, MA: MIT Press, 1971).

9. Richard K. Unterman, *Accommodating the Pedestrian* (New York: Van Nostrand Reinhold, 1984).

10. Edmund N. Bacon, *Design of Cities*, rev. ed. (New York: Penguin, 1974).

11. Carole Rifkind, *Main Street: The Face of Urban America* (New York: Harper and Row, 1977).

12. John A. Jakle, *The American Small Town: Twentieth Century Place Images* (Hamden, CT: Shoe String, 1982).

6. Streetscape and Public Space Design Guidelines

1. *Webster's II New Riverside University Dictionary* (New York: Houghton Mifflin, 1988), 119, 290, and 304.

2. William H. Whyte, *The Social Life of Small Urban Spaces* (New York: Project for Public Places, 1980), 100.

3. Whyte, *The Social Life of Small Urban Spaces*, 94.

4. The Project for Public Places (http://www.pps.org) is a contemporary organization that develops ideas and promotes high-quality public places in cities and towns around the world, continuing the work that William Whyte started.

5. National Park Service, *The Secretary of the Interior's Standards for the Treatment of Historic Properties*, http://www.nps.gov (accessed February 7, 2008).

6. National Park Service, *The Secretary of the Interior's Standards*.

7. National Park Service, Technical Preservation Services, *Historic Preservation Tax Incentives*, http://www.nps.gov (accessed February 7, 2008).

8. Interview with Paula Nye, bicycle coordinator for the Kentucky Transportation Cabinet, July 8, 2001.

9. United States Architectural and Transportation Barriers Compliance Board, *ADA and ABA Accessibility Guidelines for Buildings and Facilities*, http://www.access-board.gov/ada-aba/final.htm (accessed February 7, 2008).

10. American Association of State Highway and Transportation Officials, *Guide for the Development of Bicycle Facilities*, 3rd ed. (Washington, DC: American Association of State and Highway Transportation Officials, 1999).

11. Bruce K. Ferguson, *Porous Pavements* (Boca Raton, FL: Taylor and Francis, 2005).

12. United States Architectural and Transportation Barriers Compliance Board, *Accessibility Guidelines for Buildings and Facilities*.

13. International Dark Sky Association, http://www.darksky.org (accessed February 6, 2008).

14. James Urban, "Bringing Order to the Technical Dysfunction within the Urban Forest," *Journal of Arboriculture* 18, no. 2 (1992): 85–90.

15. Nina Bassuk and Peter Trowbridge, "Urban Islands," *Landscape Architecture* 79, no. 8 (October 1989): 130–31.

16. American Association of Nurserymen, *American Standard for Nursery Stock*, http://www.anla.org/applications/documents/docs/anlastandard2004.pdf (accessed February 7, 2008).

17. Tree Care Industry Association, *Tree, Shrub, and Other Woody Plant Maintenance—Standard Practices*, ANSI A300-2001 (New York: American National Standards Institute, 2001).

18. United States Architectural and Transportation Barriers Compliance Board, *Accessibility Guidelines for Buildings and Facilities*.

19. U.S. Department of Transportation Federal Highway Administration, *Manual on Uniform Traffic Control Devices*, http://mutcd.fhwa.dot.gov/ (accessed February 7, 2008).

Index

Industrial and service area spatial patterns, 66

Information sources: county atlases, 45–48; historic photographs, 52–54; for historic town plats, 41–45; overview, 41; Sanborn maps, 49–52

Integrated access parking model, 129–32

Integrity and authenticity, 21. *See also* authenticity

Interesting and understandable environments, 4, 38

Involvement and making sense, 4–12, 13

Isolation: in core of commercial districts, 74, 75, 78; of historic buildings by nonhistoric construction, 35–36

J

Jackson, J. B., 31, 33

Jackson, Ky., 58

Jacobs, Jane, 36

Jakle, John, 2, 199*n*1

K

Kaplan, Rachel, 4

Kaplan, Stephen, 4

Kulash, Walter, 60

L

Landmarks: for defining path segments, 114, 126, 132, 168; for orientation and legibility, 83, 114, 118, 173; overview, 30–31, *32*; prospect enhancement with, 19, *19*, 83; public art as, 31, 191

Landscape buffer ordinance, 103

Landscape buffers: for automobile corridors, 79, 168; for parking areas, 76, 80, 180, *180*; pedestrian's comfort and, 38, 76, *94–95*, 94–96, 101–4; for street corridors, 90; yards and trees as, 65, 72, 81, 109. *See also* trees

Landscapes: Bavarian theme, 27–28, *28*; and Colonial Revival movement, *25*; design issues, 70–71, 74, 114; design philosophies, 38; development over time, 41–54, *43*, *51*,

53, 56, 63–64, *63–64*; downtown area composition, 1, 2–3; in expansion zones, 76, 90–91; maintenance of, 184; preservation of, 166–67; and prospect-refuge theory, 12, 14–20, 162; residential, 81; symbolic, 33–34, 55

Land use: compact mix of, 4, 105; pedestrian routes and design of, 90–91. *See also* contemporary zones of land use and form; historic commercial district space and land use configuration; zones

Lebanon, Ohio, 56, *137*, 145–47, *146–47*, *164*

Legibility: and complexity, 4, 8–10, 39, 159; and mystery, 8–12; and orientation, 83, 114, 118, 122, 173

Lexington, Ky.: Chevy Chase shopping district, 55, 97–102, 109; and Colonial Revival movement, 24–25, *25*; connections in, 97–102, *98–101*; downtown facades, *17–18*; parking lot aesthetics, *178*, *180*; private sector signs, *194*

Library of Congress (LOC), 46–47, 49, 50, 52

Lighting: design guidelines, 181–83; historic standards, 159, 167; for parking lots and walks, 75; for pedestrian comfort, 94, 172; traffic lights, 111, 195, *196*; unity through rhythm and repetition, 31

Lingeman, Richard, 55, 89

Local strip-style developments, 77, 78

Louisville, Ky.: Bardstown Road, 97, 105–9; connections in, *105–8*, 105–9; creation of refuge, *173*; functional street furniture, *162*, *175*, *188*; pedestrian way-finding system, 197, *197*; public spaces in, *20*, *162*

Lowenthal, David, 22–26

Ludlow, Shropshire, England, *9*

Lynch, Kevin, 30–31, 114

M

Madison, Wisc., *174*

Main Street program, 2, 33–34, 56, 128

Main Street Revisited (Francaviglia), 25–26